Easy Origami

Folded Fun for All Ages

Debora Argueta

STERLING INNOVATION
New York

STERLING INNOVATION
New York

An Imprint of Sterling Publishing
387 Park Avenue South
New York, NY 10016

Photography by Christopher C. Bain

ISBN 978-1-4027-9617-3

This book is part of the *Easy Origami* kit and is not to be sold separately.

Distributed in Canada by Sterling Publishing
c/o Canadian Manda Group, 165 Dufferin Street
Toronto, Ontario, Canada M6K 3H6
Distributed in the United Kingdom by GMC Distribution Services
Castle Place, 166 High Street, Lewes, East Sussex, England BN7 1XU
Distributed in Australia by Capricorn Link (Australia) Pty. Ltd.
P.O. Box 704, Windsor, NSW 2756, Australia

For information about custom editions, special sales, and premium and corporate purchases, please contact Sterling Special Sales at 800-805-5489 or specialsales@sterlingpublishing.com.

Manufactured in China

Lot #
4 6 8 10 9 7 5
09/13

www.sterlingpublishing.com

About the Author

Debora was born in Brazil, but she didn't live there for very long. With pictures of a snow-covered college campus and the promise of adventure and higher education, her father uprooted Debora, her mother, and her two brothers and brought them to the United States when Debora was five. She grew up in a small town in central Massachusetts where she learned to appreciate the value of a quiet and peaceful life.

In 2006 Debora began making origami mobiles and selling them through her website HangingOrigami.com. Debora's graduate studies took her to Chicago where she had the opportunity to visit great museums and study mobiles by the famous American sculptor Alexander Calder, as well as those by Jan R. Carson.

Debora recently graduated from medical school and is excited about her career as a physician in which her art will continually touch her patients' lives. She lives in central Massachusetts with her husband and two young children.

Contents

Introduction

Origami, the Japanese art of paper folding, has been around for centuries. All you need to enjoy it is a piece of paper, some instruction, and a little imagination.

This book shows you how to fold simple traditional and original origami models. What's nice about folding origami models is that they are easy to learn and memorize. By memorizing the steps, you get the freedom to fold anywhere you go, and you don't even need to have origami paper at hand. Take-out menus, gum wrappers, Post-it notes, fliers, program bulletins, leaflets, or any other scrap pieces of paper can be cut into the right shapes and folded into origami models. It's fun to turn a flat, boring piece of paper into a three-dimensional model that can be played with, given as a gift, or used as a decoration.

Another fun aspect of origami is that since it's a quiet hobby, you can fold anywhere without disturbing anyone. It provides you with a nice way to pass the time in the car, bus, train, or plane, and helps calm your nerves in a waiting room. With enough practice, you'll find that you can keep your fingers busy folding while your mind is free to wander. Paper folding is so quick and easy that you can fit it into your day whenever you have a couple of minutes to spare (a traditional paper crane takes just two to seven minutes to fold, depending on your level of experience). Take the knowledge and skills you acquire from this book and apply them towards all your future folding endeavors, whether you're following more complex diagrams, or creating your own original models.

Getting Started

Before you start to fold your first origami models, read through this section to familiarize yourself with the tools, symbols, folding techniques, and origami bases used in this book. Practice the basic folding techniques and bases on scrap paper squares until you feel comfortable executing them.

Tools You'll Need

BONE FOLDER: Use a bone folder to make sharp creases in the paper you fold. Bone folders must be used against a hard surface such as a table, desk, or a hardcover book. You can find bone folders in art supply stores, craft stores, and specialty paper shops.

GLITTER: You can use glitter to add some sparkle to any model. I love using fine glitter on origami butterflies. Depending on what sort of glitter design you'd like on your butterfly wings or other origami model, there are several different application methods you can try. Using a glue bottle with a fine tip, draw designs directly on the origami model and then sprinkle the glitter on the model. You can also use a glue pen to draw on the origami model, or use a paintbrush to brush glue onto the model. Remember to work fast so the glue doesn't dry before you apply the glitter. To avoid unsightly clumps, always use a thin layer of glue when you're adding glitter to your origami model.

GLUE: I recommend clear-drying, permanent white craft glue for gluing paper. One exception:

I have found that a small amount of super glue works pretty well for gluing the flowers together—it dries very quickly, which means less time holding the flower petals together.

PAPER: Origami paper is thinner than ordinary office paper. This thinness allows you to add many folds to a small model without it becoming bulky. Foil origami paper is an excellent alternative when folding models that tend to get bulky when made with regular origami paper. Many craft stores sell 150mm square sheets of origami paper (basically 6x6-inch squares), but sometimes you need other sizes too. You can buy smaller sheets or cut your large squares into smaller ones as needed using scissors or a paper trimmer (see sidebar).

PAPER TRIMMER: I like to use a paper trimmer to cut origami paper because it makes straight cuts. Paper trimmers in a wide range of sizes and prices can be found at craft stores or office supply stores.

Simple, portable paper trimmers have a small blade that glides along a plastic track. Guillotine paper trimmers may be more bulky and dangerous, but you are able to cut more sheets at once. Also,

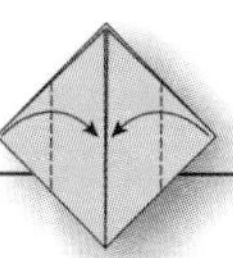

PAPER TRIMMING TIPS: Some of the origami models in this book require pieces of paper that are smaller than 6x6 inches. In those cases, take a 6x6-inch sheet and cut it into one 4¾x4¾-inch sheet or four 3x3-inch sheets. Since origami paper isn't exactly 6x6 inches (it's slightly smaller), you have to find the halfway point on your origami paper by one of two methods: You can use a ruler to measure out the midpoint of your large sheet of paper, mark it, and slice the paper. Or you can bend the paper gently as if you were going to fold your square into two rectangles, and just make a small crease along the edge of the paper. Once you've created that small crease, open the paper, lay it on the paper trimmer's work surface, lining up the crease with the path of the blade, and slice. Next, take one rectangle, bend it and crease it as you did for the first cut, lay one rectangle on top of the other on the trimmer, and slice. Choose the method that works best for you.

their larger work surface allows for more precise measurements and straighter cuts.

Pens or Markers: Not every sheet of origami paper will have all the details that you might want for your final model. You may want to add spots to your giraffe, stripes to your zebra, or eyes to the animals. Use a pen or marker to create the effect you want.

Scissors: Sharp scissors are sometimes needed for small precision cuts. For small cuts I like using the tiny scissors from a Swiss army knife because they're so sharp and precise.

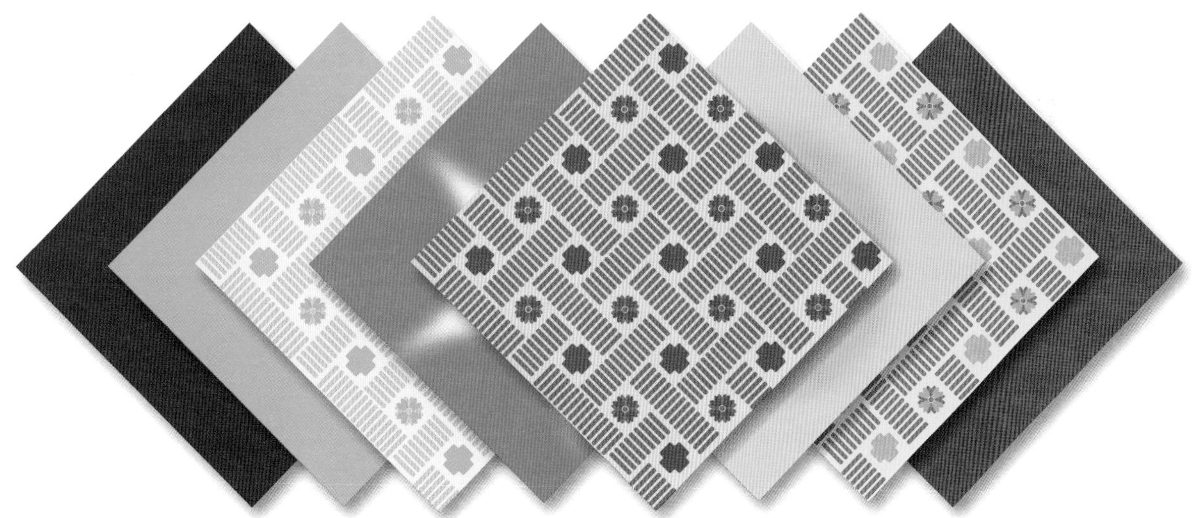

Symbols

Here are some symbols you'll need to be familiar with before folding. If you're new to origami, look over this page carefully. Otherwise, you can just use this guide as a quick reference when you don't remember what a symbol means.

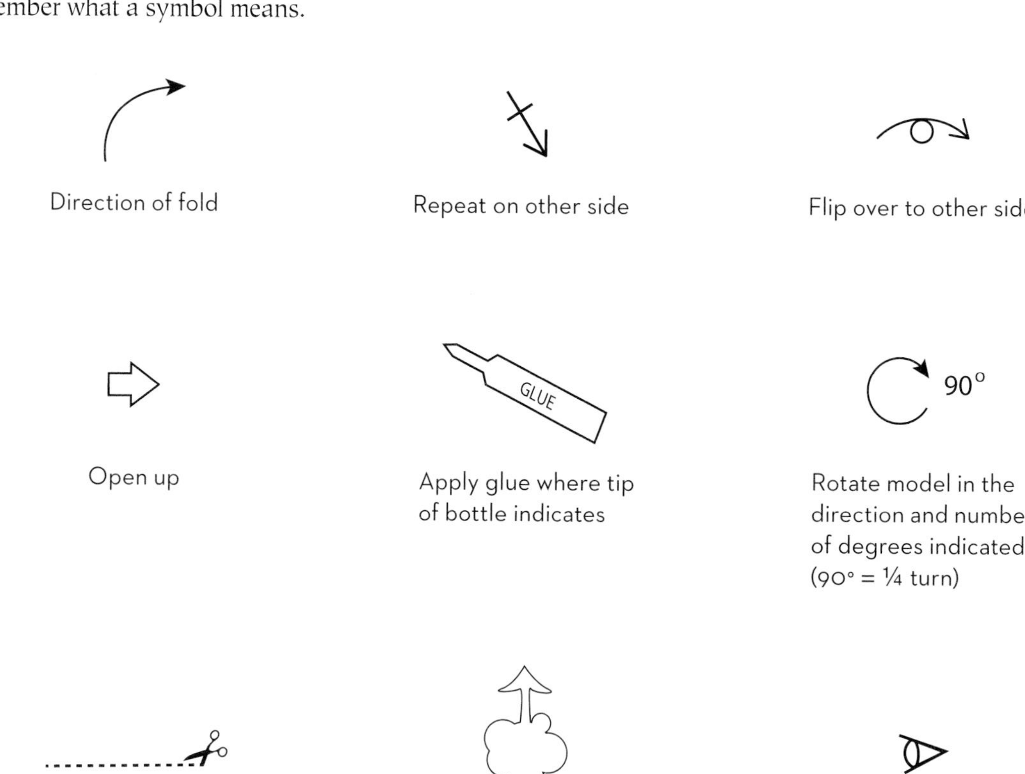

Direction of fold

Repeat on other side

Flip over to other side

Open up

Apply glue where tip of bottle indicates

Rotate model in the direction and number of degrees indicated (90° = ¼ turn)

Cut along dashed line

Inflate with air

Look at model from point of view indicated by side profile of eye

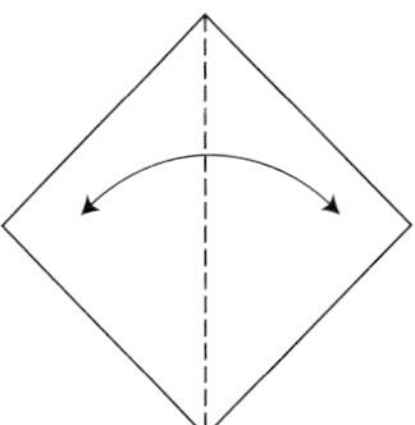

Fold and unfold to make a crease

The solid line indicates a crease in the paper

Push here

Squash fold here

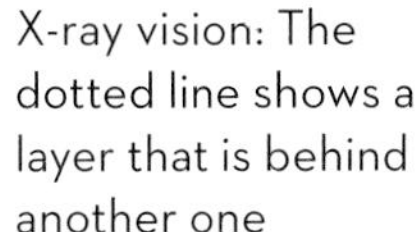

X-ray vision: The dotted line shows a layer that is behind another one

Mountain fold: The dot-dash line indicates folding the paper away from you to make a "mountain"

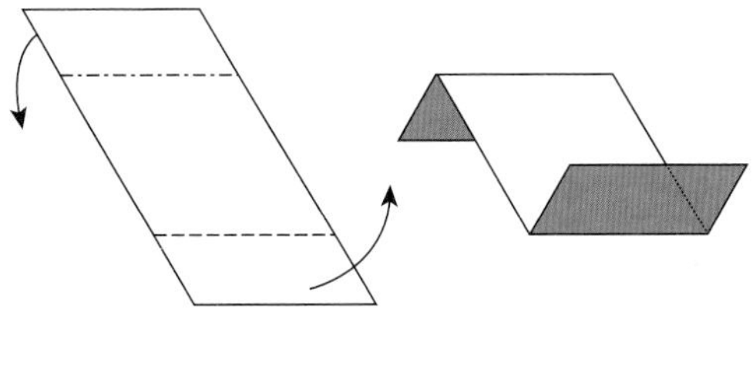

Pleat fold: Mountain fold and valley fold two sequential sections to create a "pleat"

Valley fold: The dash line indicates folding the paper toward you to make a "valley"

Folding Techniques

These are the basic origami folds used to make the projects in this book and many other origami models. If you're new to origami it might take you a few tries to master them. Work with scrap paper squares to start.

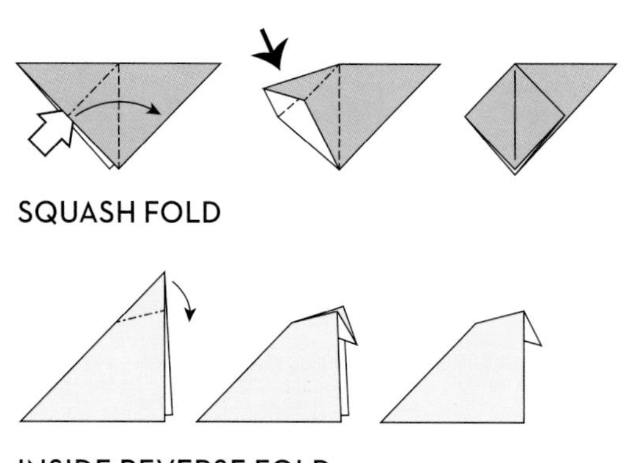

SQUASH FOLD

INSIDE REVERSE FOLD

Squash fold: Make a valley fold down the center. Open up the front layer and press where indicated by the black arrow creating two mountain folds. Refold along the valley fold line and flatten.

Inside reverse fold: Mountain fold to crease paper. Push tip in to reverse the fold. Flatten the model.

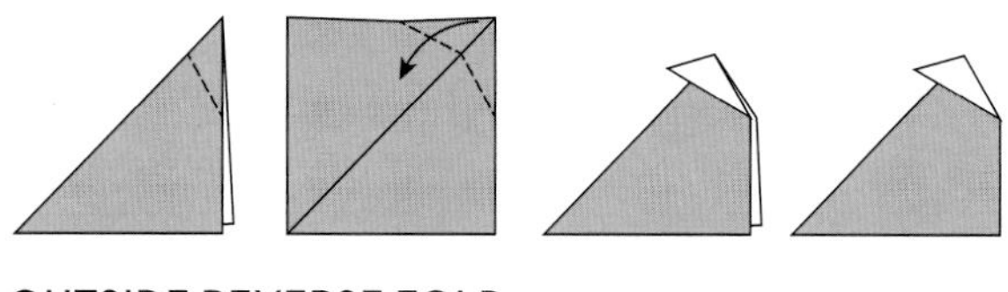

OUTSIDE REVERSE FOLD

Outside reverse fold: Valley fold to crease paper. Open up the model and fold tip back along valley fold crease while re-closing model, then flatten the model.

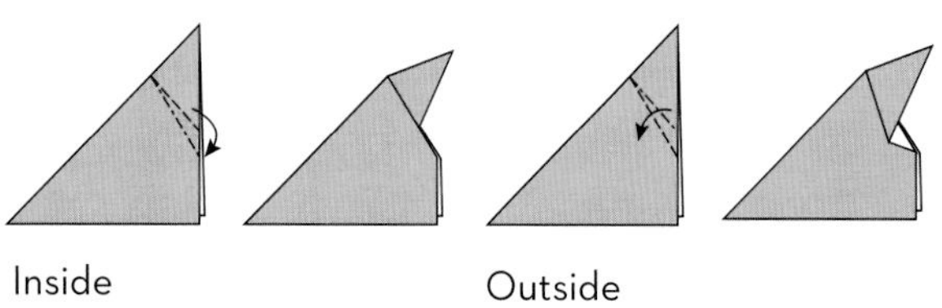

Inside

Outside

CRIMP FOLD

Crimp fold: Make mountain and valley folds as indicated, then collapse along those creases. The first two diagrams illustrate an inside crimp fold; the second two show an outside crimp fold.

Petal fold: This fold is used to create both the bird and frog bases discussed in the next section. Fold and unfold along all valley fold marks, then lift top layer only. Open up top layer and refold along previously made creases. This forms a "petal" of paper.

PETAL FOLD

Sink fold: Begin with a waterbomb base (see page 13), valley fold and unfold a small triangle on top, then open the sheet up. Re-crease the folds you just made into mountain folds. Collapse sheet back into waterbomb base. Push where the black arrowhead indicates to sink the tip inside along the creases you made.

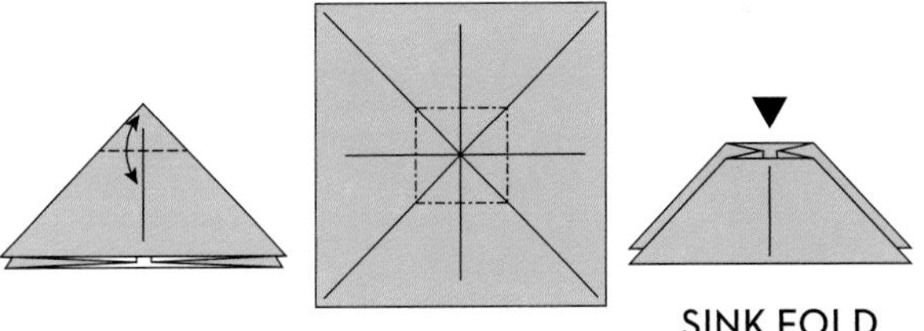

SINK FOLD

Rabbit ear: Fold and unfold along all valley fold marks. Collapse along those creases by pushing where the black arrowheads indicate, and swing the upper left tip of the sheet down so it lies along the center crease. This forms a "rabbit ear" on your model.

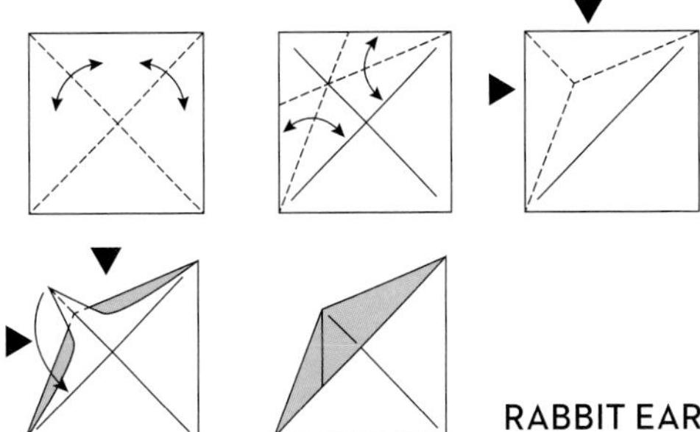

RABBIT EAR

Origami Bases

Many origami models start with the same first steps that form what is known as a base. There are several commonly used bases that form the foundation for a variety of models. A bird base, for example, can go on to become a bird, a fish, or a star. Rather than repeating these steps in the instructions for each model, they are all grouped here for quick and easy reference..

SQUARE BASE

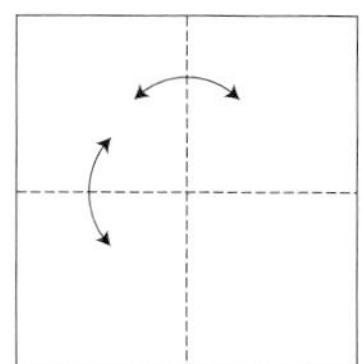

1. Valley fold and unfold.

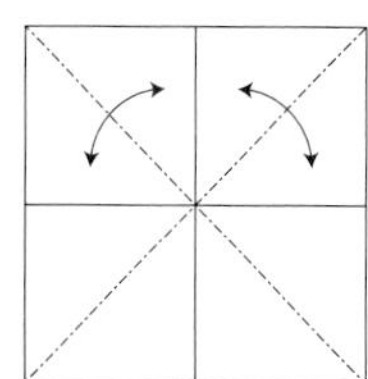

2. Mountain fold and unfold. Turn over.

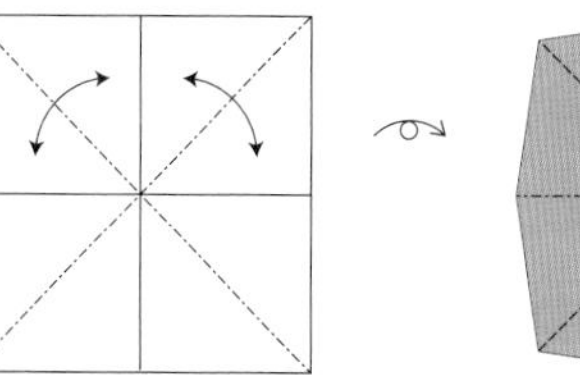

3. Collapse model along creases.

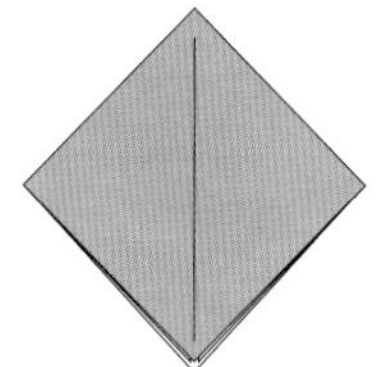

4. Completed square base.

BIRD BASE

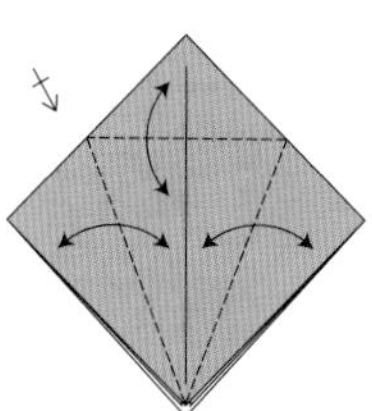

1. Begin with square base (above). Valley fold and unfold, repeat on back side.

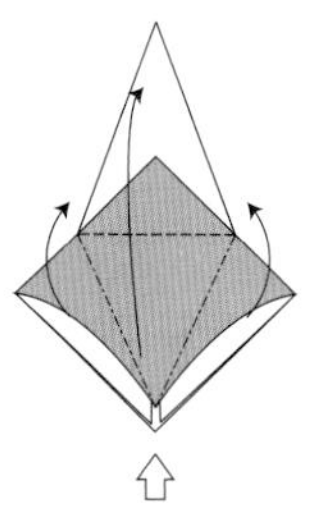

2. Open up and petal fold top layer.

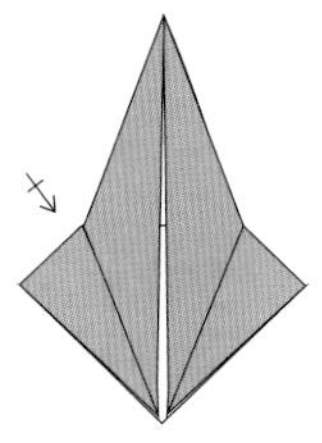

3. Repeat petal fold on back side.

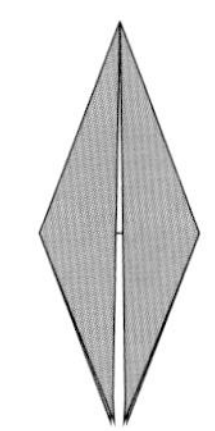

4. Completed bird base.

Waterbomb Base

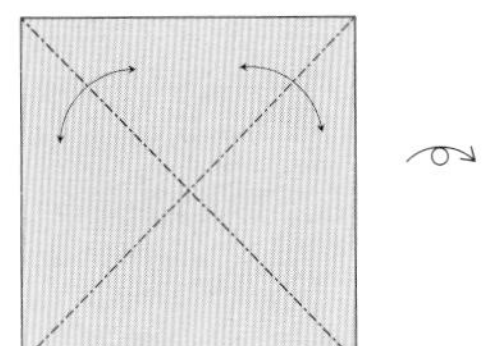

1. Mountain fold and unfold. Turn over.

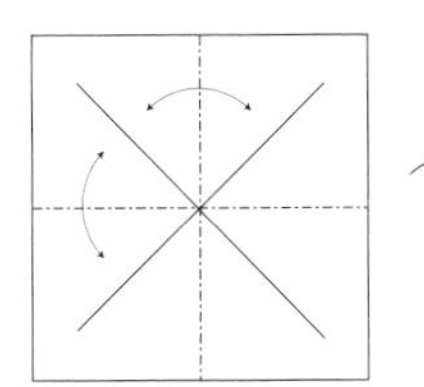

2. Mountain fold and unfold. Turn over.

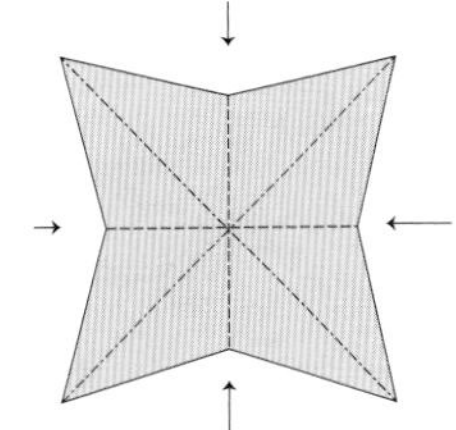

3. Collapse paper along creases.

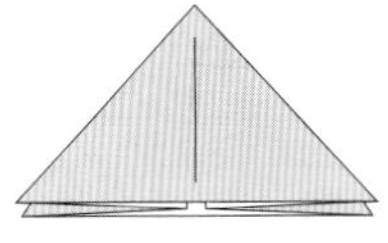

4. Completed waterbomb base.

Diamond Base

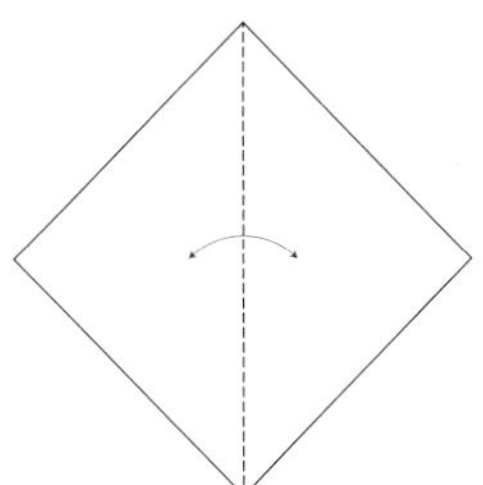

1. Valley fold and unfold.

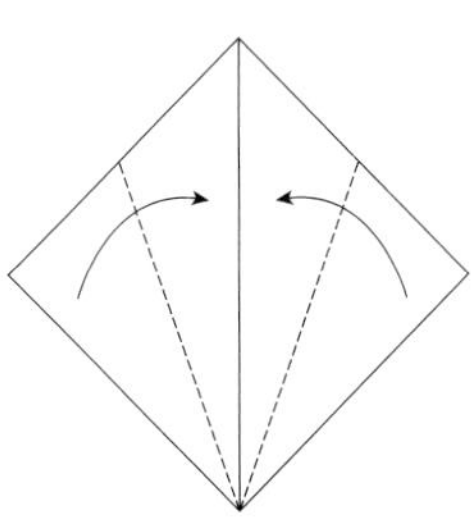

2. Valley fold to center.

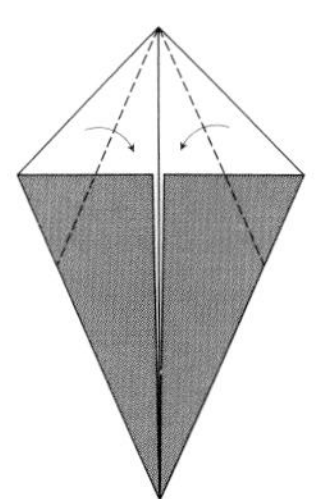

3. Valley fold to center.

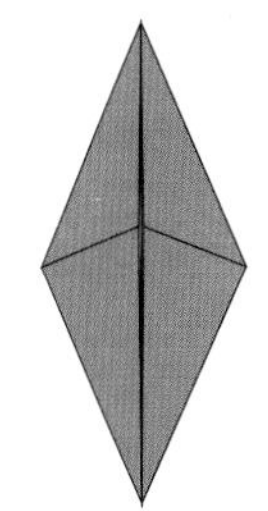

4. Completed diamond base.

Fish Base

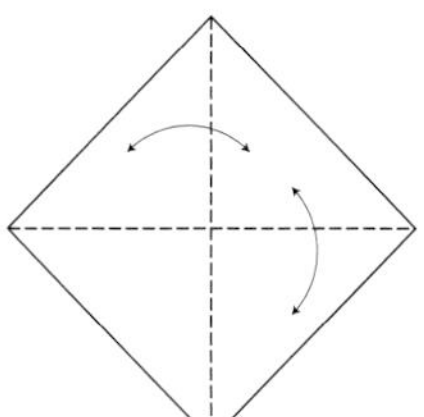

1. Valley fold and unfold.

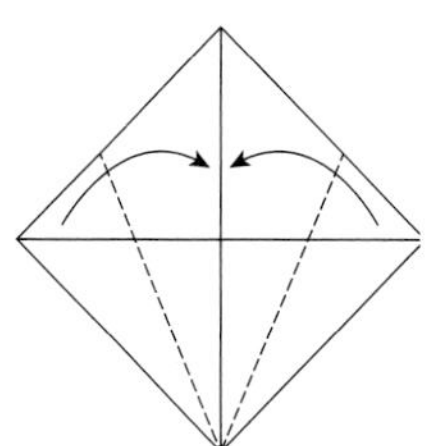

2. Valley fold to center.

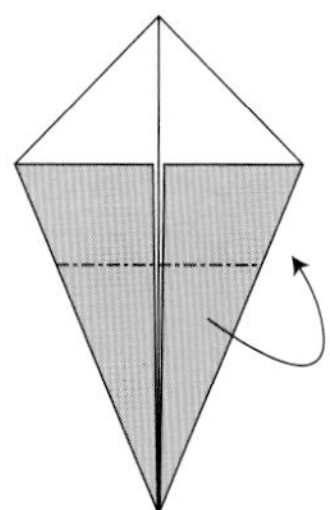

3. Mountain fold to back.

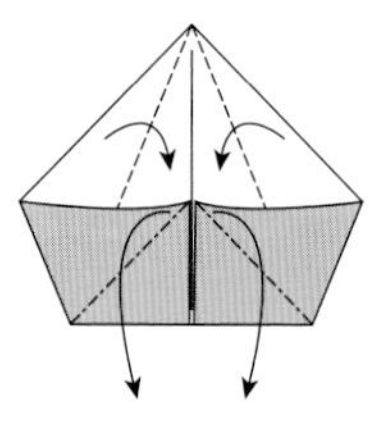

4. Pull top layer down and valley fold sides in to center.

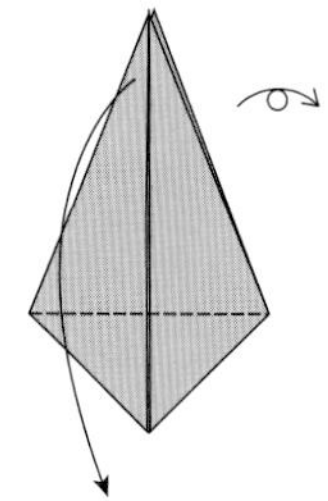

5. Valley fold down top flap only. Turn over.

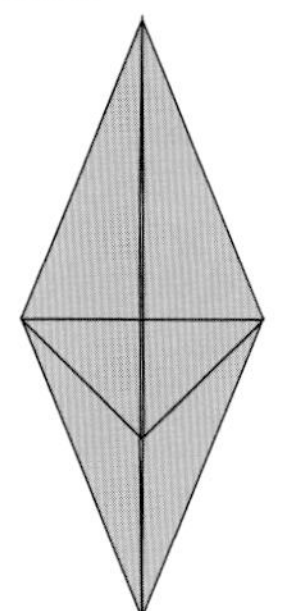

6. Completed fish base.

Blintz Base

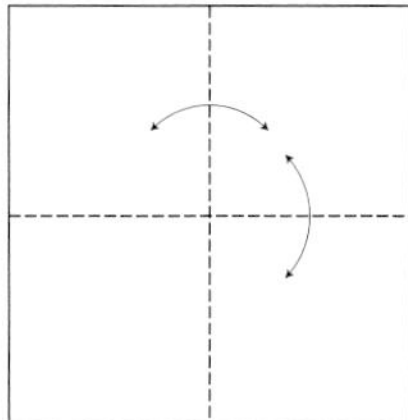

1. Valley fold and unfold.

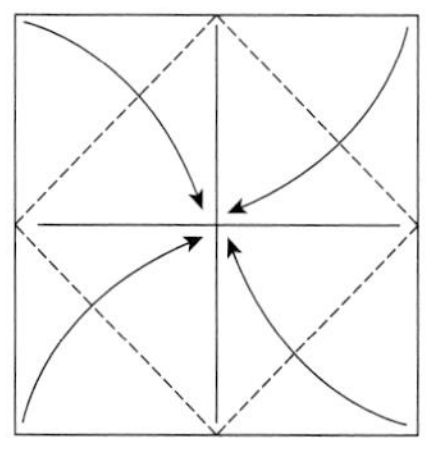

2. Valley fold all corners to center.

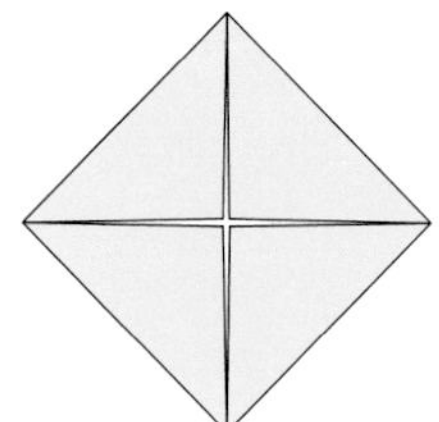

3. Completed blintz base.

Frog Base

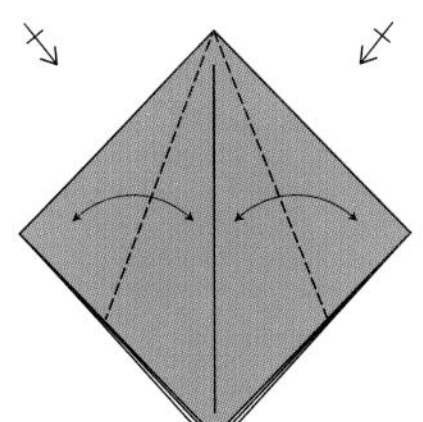

1. Begin with a square base. Valley fold and unfold the top layer to the center crease. Repeat on other side.

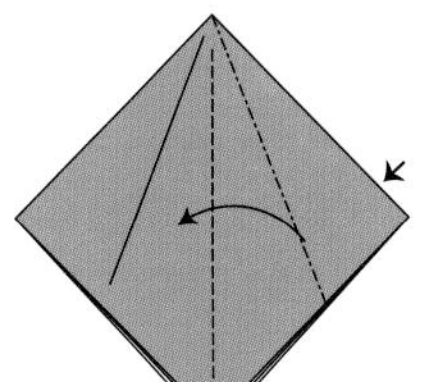

2. Squash fold along the creases made in the previous step.

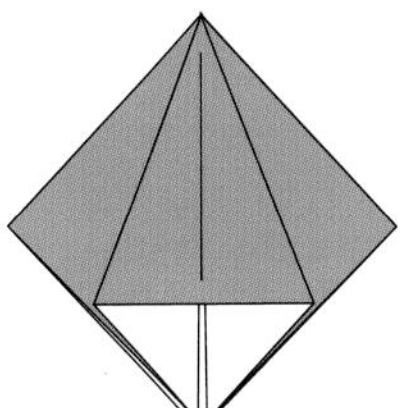

3. Repeat the squash fold on every face of the model.

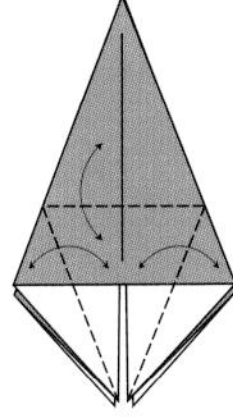

4. Valley fold and unfold along these lines. Repeat on all faces of the model.

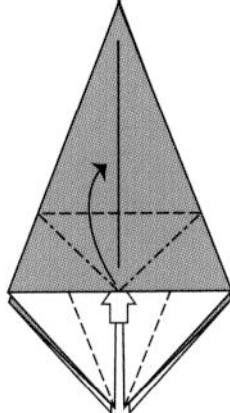

5. Petal fold.

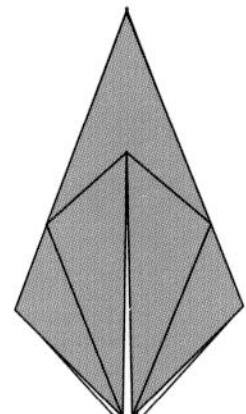

6. Repeat petal fold on all faces of the model.

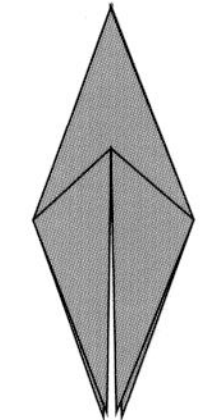

7. Completed frog base.

PEACE CRANE

What to Use

- **6x6-inch paper =** 3-inch crane
- **3x3-inch paper =** 1½-inch crane
- **Base required:** bird (see page 12)
- **Paper required:** one sheet

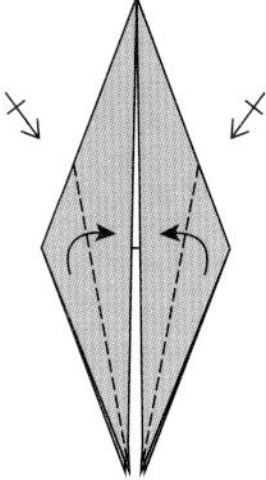

1. Starting with a bird base, valley fold sides of top layer only. Repeat on the other side.

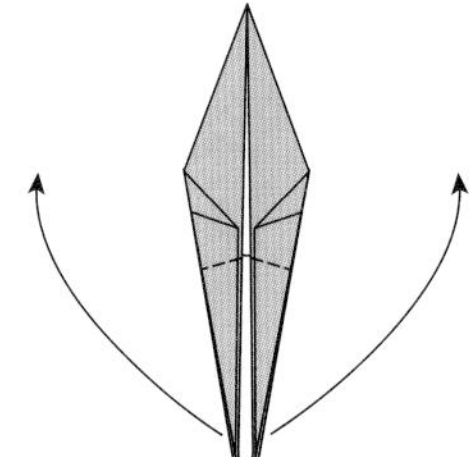

2. Inside reverse fold to raise head and tail sections.

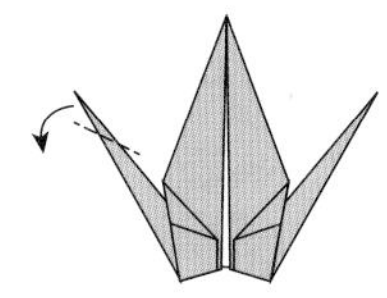

3. Inside reverse fold to form beak.

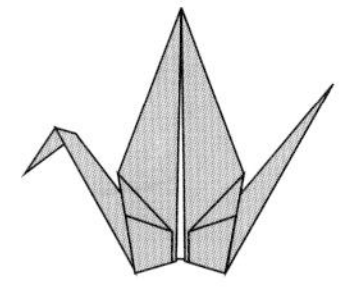

4. Completed crane.

BUTTERFLY

What to Use

- **6x6-inch paper =** 5-inch butterfly
- **3x3-inch paper =** 2½-inch butterfly
- **Base required:** waterbomb (see page 13)
- **Paper required:** one sheet

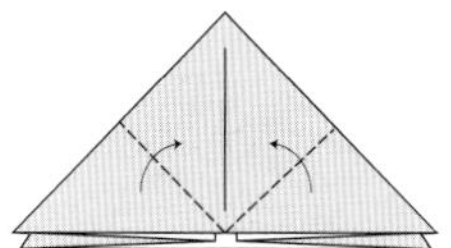

1. Starting with a waterbomb base, valley fold top layer only.

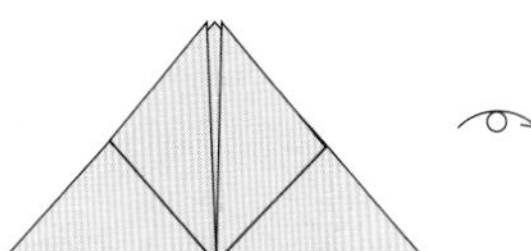

2. Flip model over.

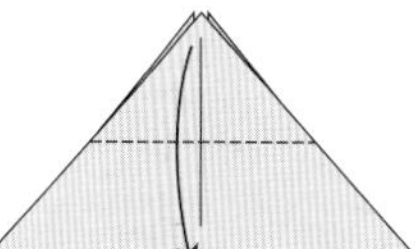

3. Valley fold front layer down far enough so that a small triangle of paper hangs over the bottom edge to form the head.

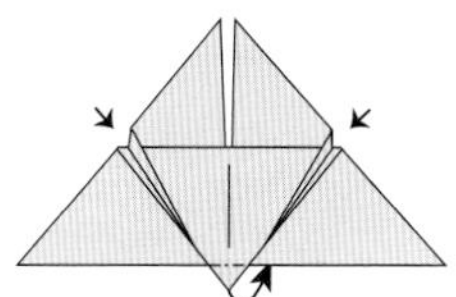

4. Squash fold these open layers flat. Mountain fold the butterfly's head.

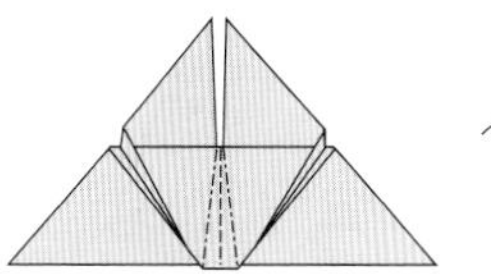

5. Mountain fold and valley fold. Flip model over and turn it 180°.

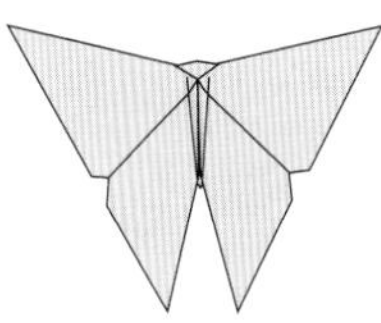

6. Completed butterfly.

FLOWER

What to Use

- **6x6-inch paper =** 3½-inch flower
- **3x3-inch paper =** 2-inch flower
- **Base required:** bird (see page 12)
- **Paper required:** five sheets

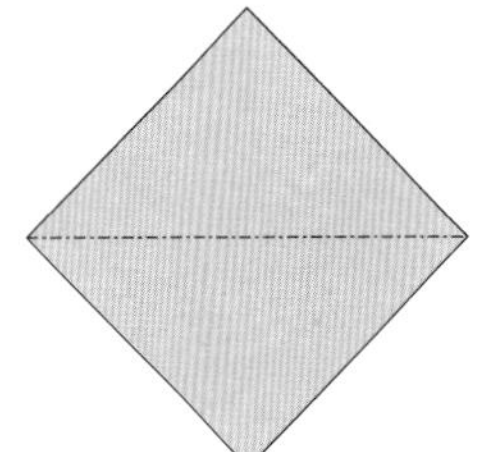

1. Mountain fold so colored side is out.

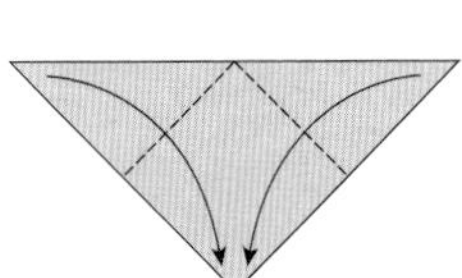

2. Valley fold corners to center.

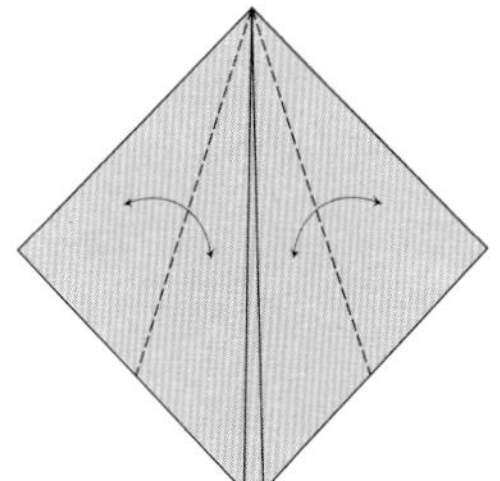

3. Valley fold and unfold top flaps only.

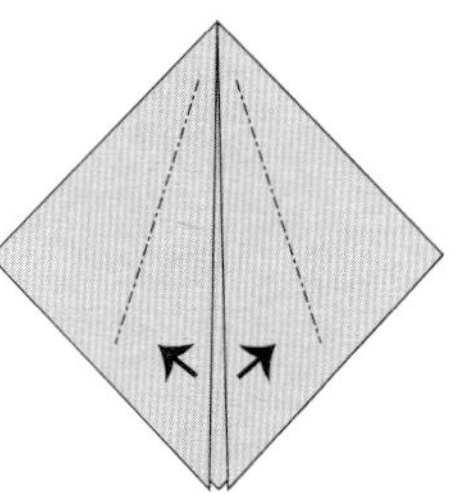

4. Squash fold both sides open along the creases you just made.

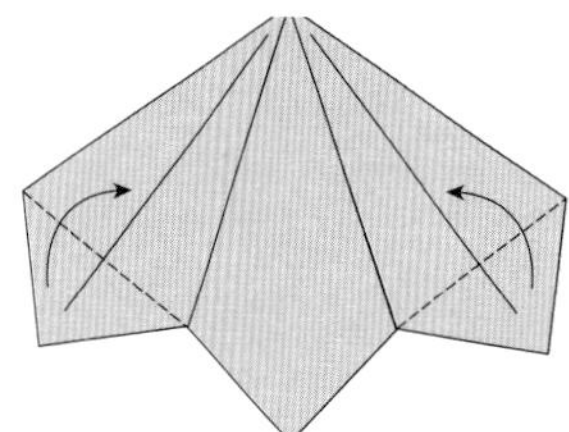

5. Valley fold tips so that white side of paper is exposed.

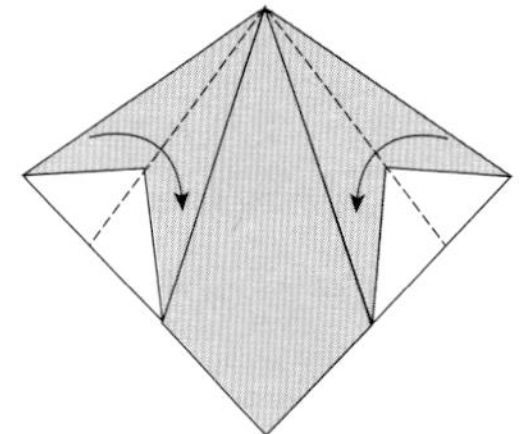

6. Valley fold side sections along creases.

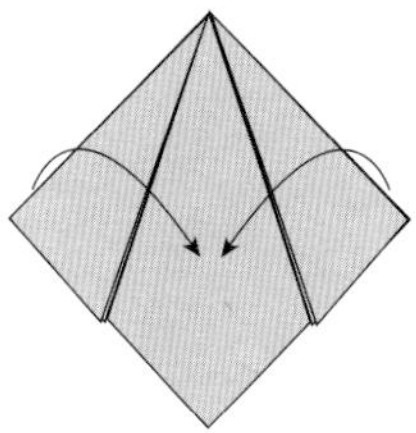

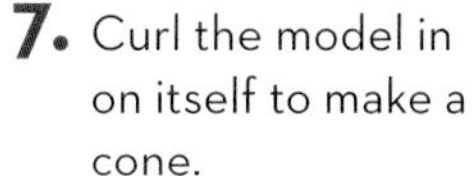

7. Curl the model in on itself to make a cone.

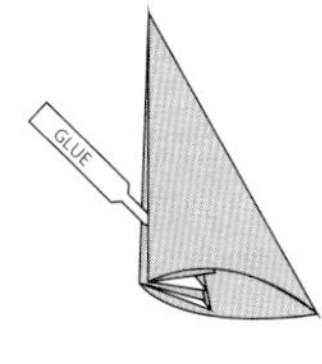

8. Glue the two sides of the cone together. Set aside the flower unit and make four more.

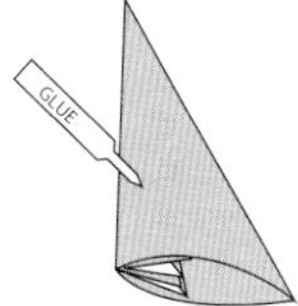

9. Apply glue to one side of a flower unit near the seam as shown and press another flower unit into place next to it, with seams matching. Repeat for the remaining units to form one complete flower with five petals.

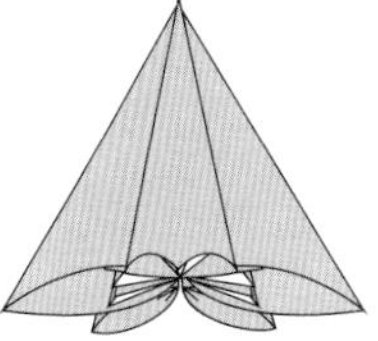

10. Completed flower.

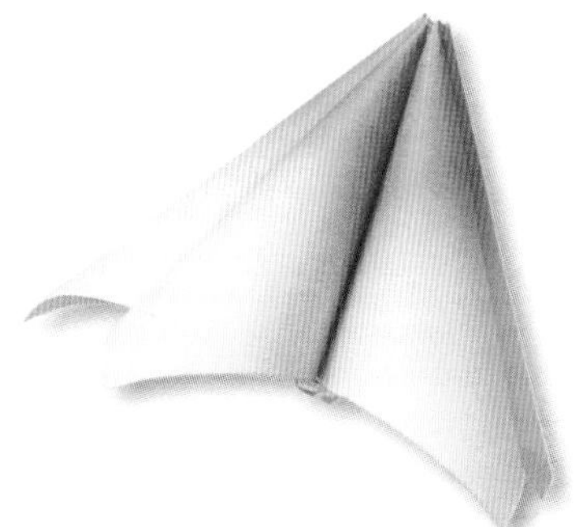

Tip: *Flowers look really nice when you use paper that has a color gradient, or two or three color gradients, on the same sheet.*

SNOWFLAKE

What to Use

- **6x6-inch paper =** 7-inch snowflake
- **3x3-inch paper =** $3\frac{1}{2}$-inch snowflake
- **Paper required:** six sheets of the same size paper

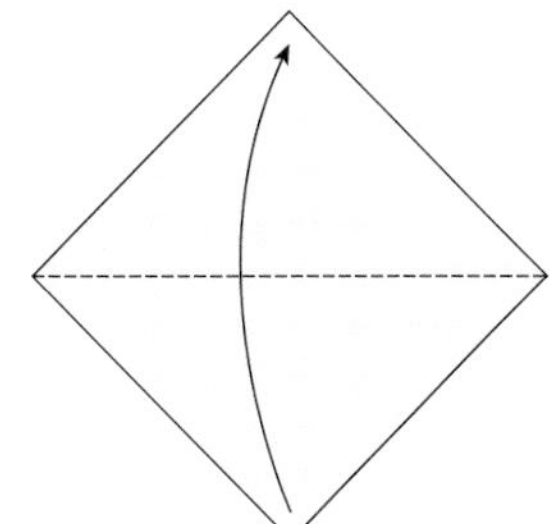

1. Valley fold paper in half.

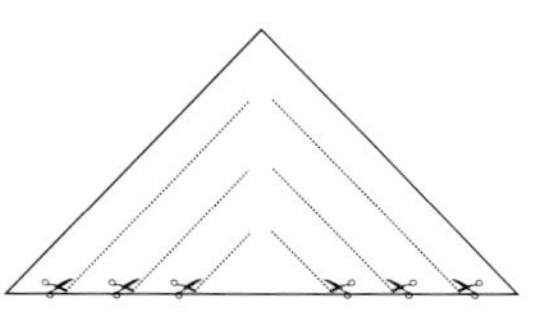

2. Cut three lines on each side, but do not cut all the way to the center. Open up sheet.

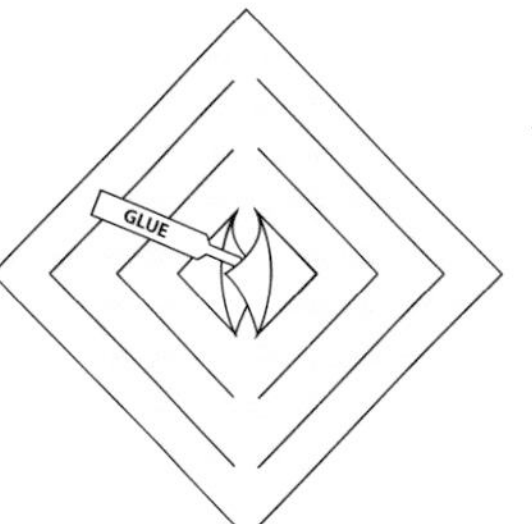

3. Curl the two center triangles toward each other to form a tube. Glue or tape the ends together.

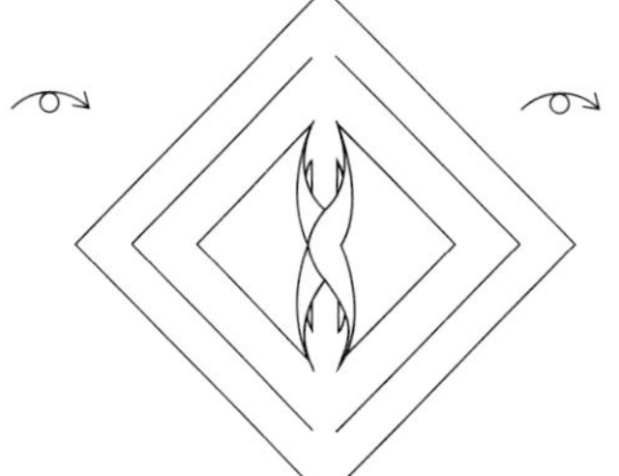

4. On the other side, curl the next section in to form a bigger tube. Tape or glue the ends together.

5. Repeat Steps 3 and 4 for the next two sections to make a unit like this. Make five more units.

6. Glue or tape the center points of three units together. Repeat with the three remaining units.

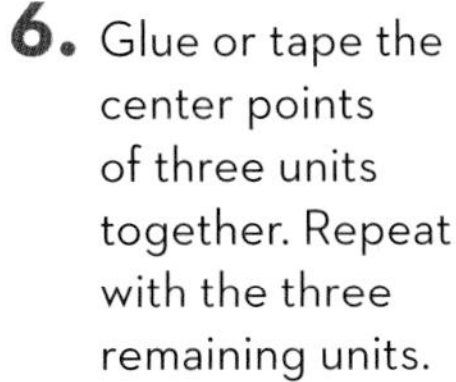

7. Glue or tape both groups of three together. Also place a dot of glue at each point where the individual units touch so the snowflake maintains its shape.

8. The snowflake can also be one solid color by using paper that is the same on both sides.

9. Completed snowflake.

GIRAFFE

What to Use

- **6x6-inch paper =** 4½-inch giraffe
- **3x3-inch paper =** 2¼-inch giraffe
- **Base required:** fish (see page 14)
- **Paper required:** one sheet

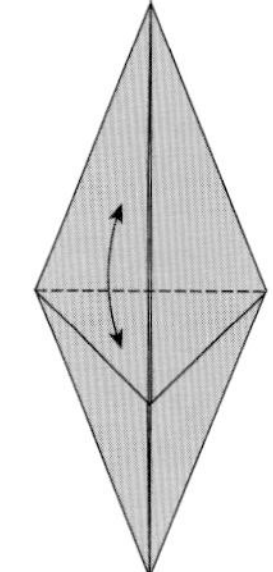

1. Starting with a fish base, valley fold and unfold to crease well. Turn model 90°.

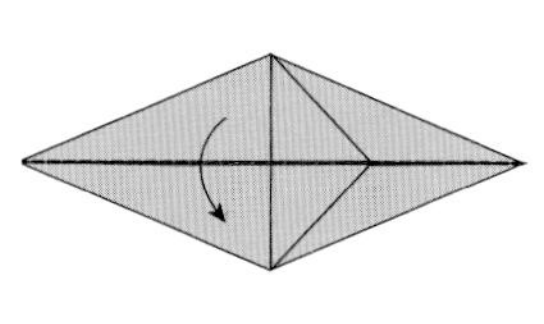

2. Valley fold entire model lengthwise along the center crease.

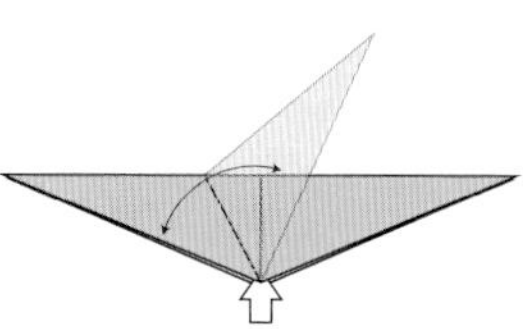

3. Mountain fold the model as shown. Crease well and open model back up.

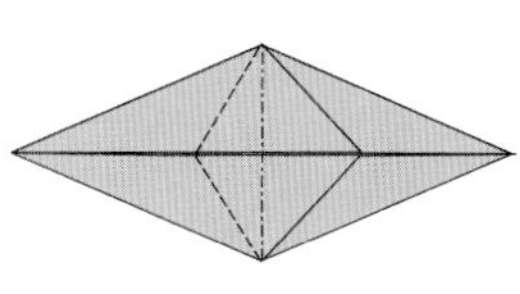

4. Using creases you just made, mountain and valley fold model.

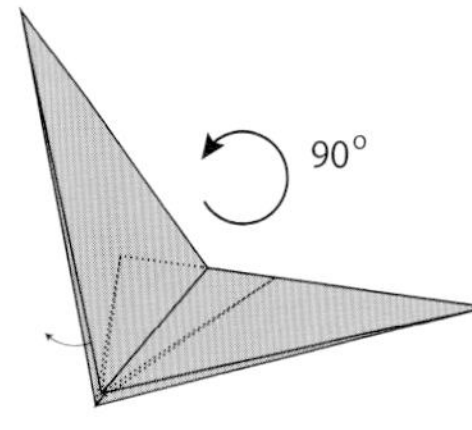

5. Pull the two short flaps out from inside the model, and rotate model 90°.

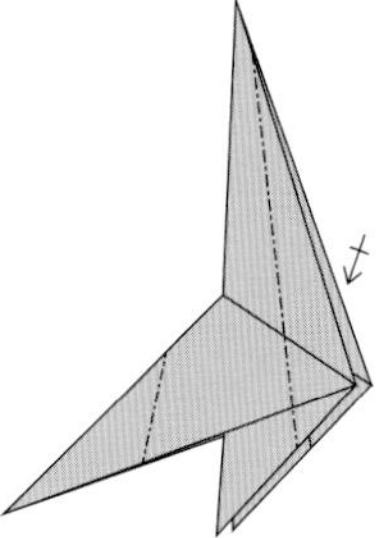

6. Inside reverse fold the hind leg down, and narrow the neck by mountain folding the front and back flaps in.

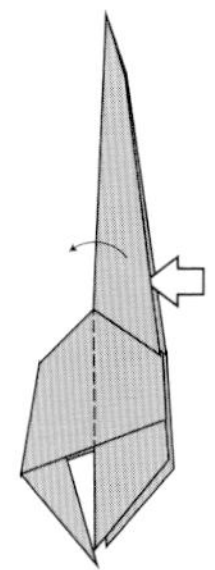

7. Open up front flap only.

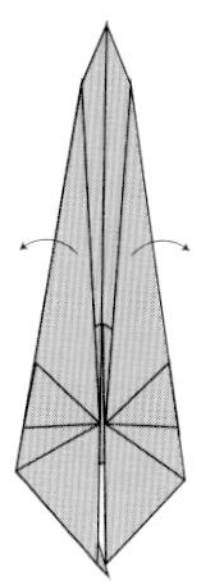

8. Open up side flaps.

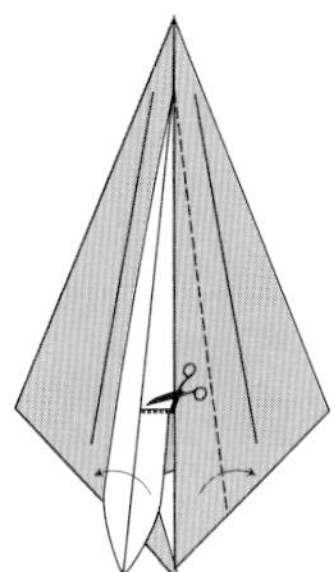

9. Valley fold the top flap first; the back flap will follow. Cut below the base of the neck so the top and back flaps can fold together.

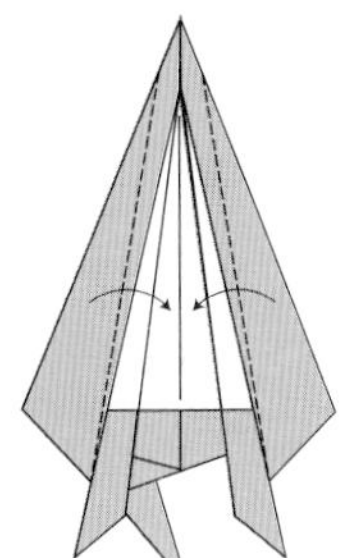

10. Valley fold sides back in.

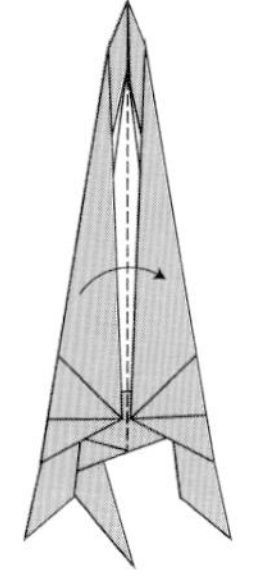

11. Valley fold along center crease.

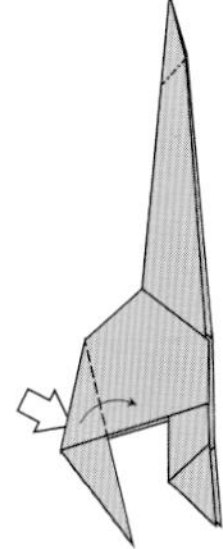

12. Outside reverse fold hind legs and inside reverse fold head.

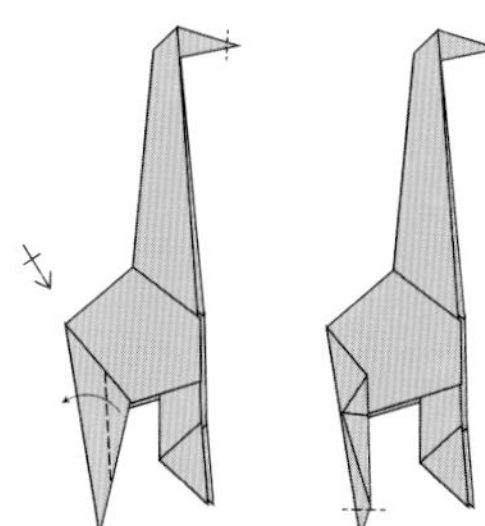

13. Valley fold back legs on both sides. Then, inside reverse fold back feet only.

LION

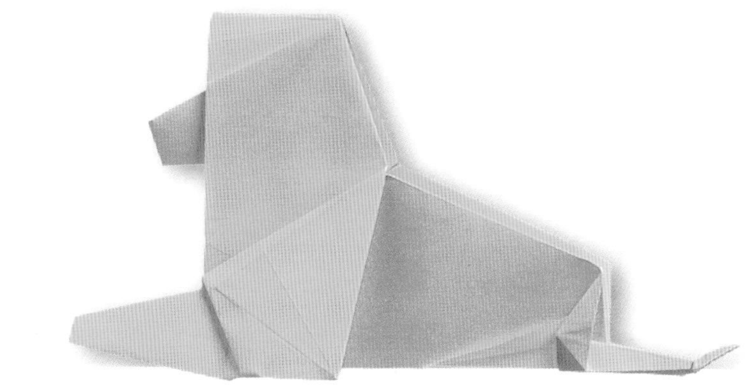

What to Use

- **6x6-inch paper =** 4-inch lion
- **3x3-inch paper =** 2-inch lion
- **Base required:** fish (see page 14)
- **Paper required:** one sheet

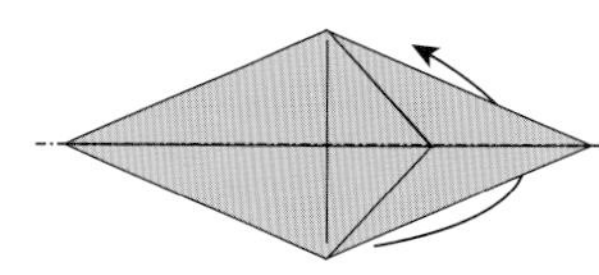

1. Starting with the fish base, mountain fold up along center crease.

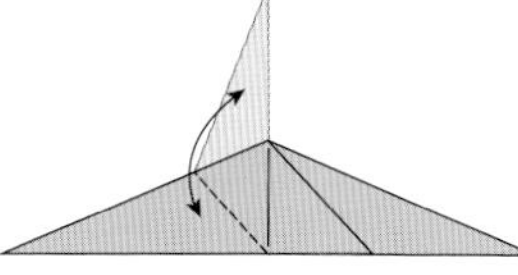

2. Valley fold and unfold. Crease well.

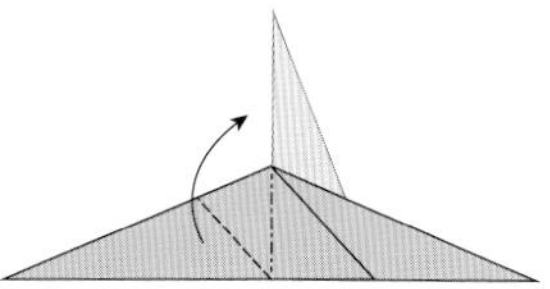

3. Crimp fold along the creases you made in Step 2.

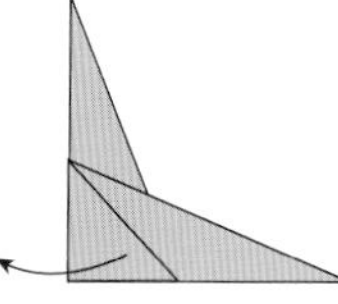

4. Unfold leg flap.

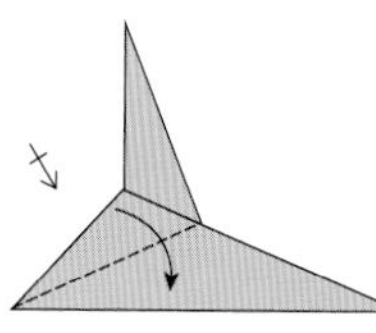

5. Valley fold to narrow the leg and repeat on the other side.

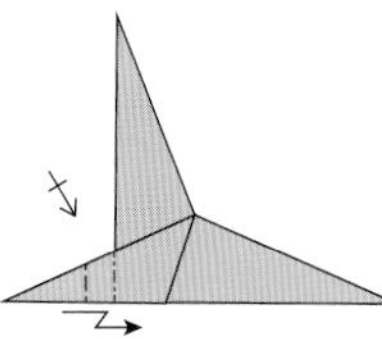

6. Crease first and then pleat fold the leg along the creases you just made. Repeat on other side.

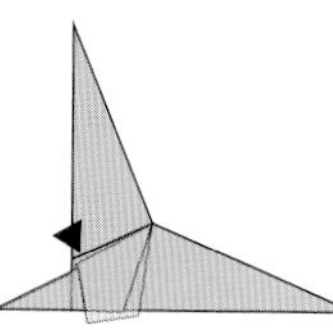

7. Push down on top of the leg until you displace the top crease enough to give the elbow joint a nice angle.

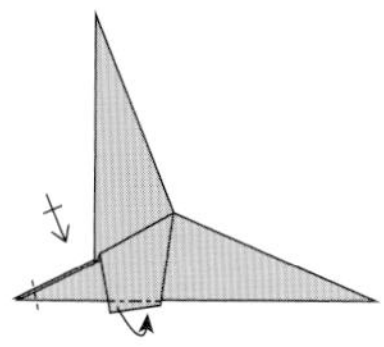

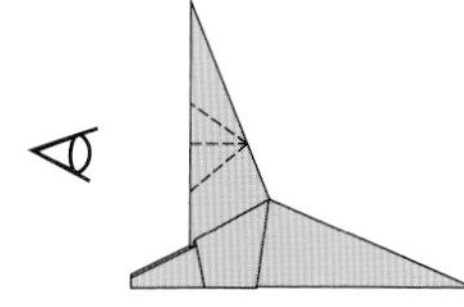

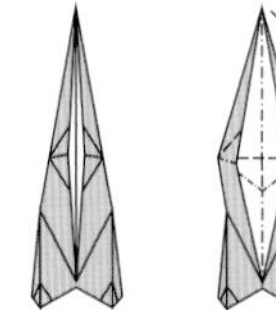

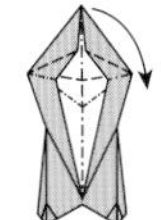

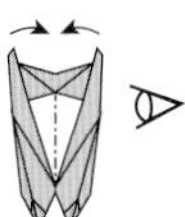

8. Mountain fold to tuck extra leg flap under leg and fold toes under. Repeat on other side.

9. Valley fold and unfold as shown to form three creases. Then turn lion so you are looking directly into his face.

10. Push on the tip of the lion's head to collapse it down, making sure each mountain or valley fold is going in the right direction.

11. Bring sides of head together and rotate lion back to side profile.

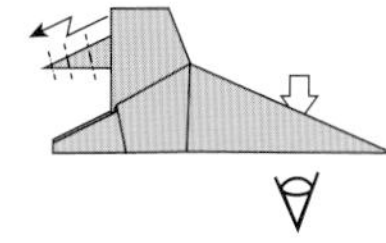

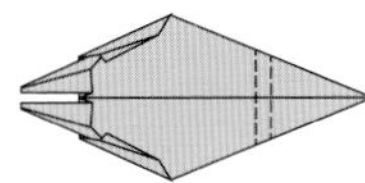

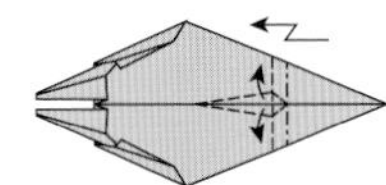

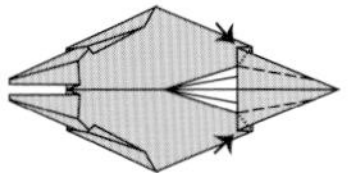

12. Pleat fold the lion's face to create a little nose that can only be seen from the front, then open up the rear end slightly and rotate model so you are looking at it from the underside.

13. Fold and unfold along these lines to form creases.

14. Pleat fold along the creases you made in Step 13, opening up to fold two long triangles to form hind legs.

15. Squash fold to narrow the tail.

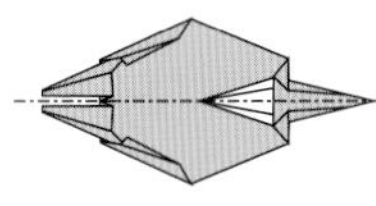

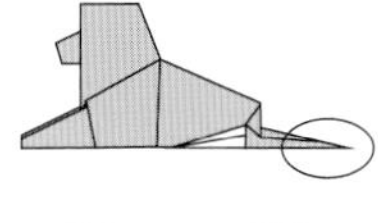

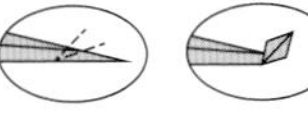

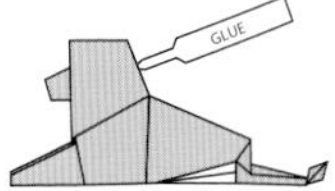

16. Mountain fold model along center crease to return it to its original position.

17. Crimp fold to form tuft of hair on lion's tail.

18. Apply a small amount of glue inside the back of the lion's head to hold it together.

ZEBRA

What to Use

- **6x6-inch and 5½ x 5½-inch paper =** 4½-inch zebra
- **3x3-inch and 2¾ x 2¾ inch paper =** 2¾-inch zebra
- **Bases required:** fish (see page 14)
- **Paper required:** two sheets of paper; one trimmed slightly smaller than the other (use paper with zebra stripes, if you have some)

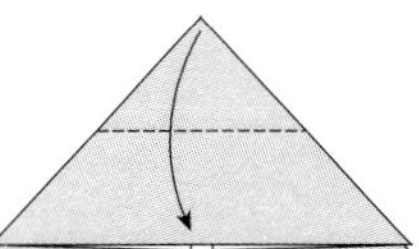

1. Make the body: Using the larger paper and starting with a waterbomb base, valley fold the top half down.

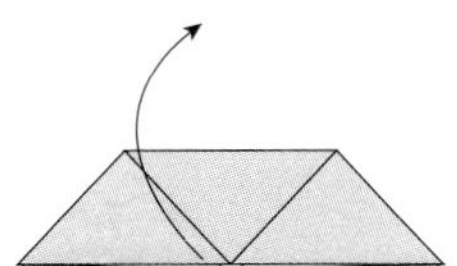

2. Lift front layer and open up model, squash folding the model flat.

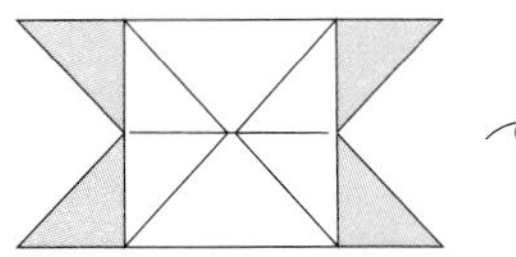

3. Flip the model over.

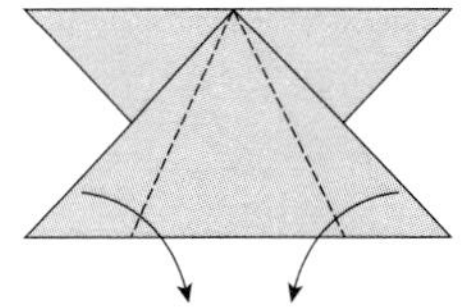

4. Valley fold lower tips down as far as they go.

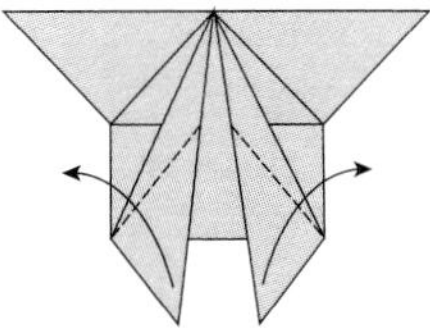

5. Valley fold up and out.

6. Valley fold down.

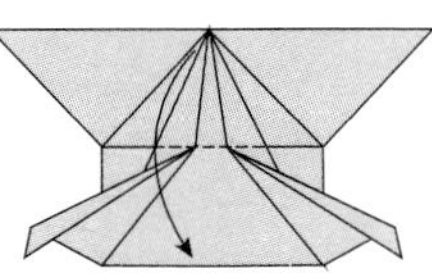

7. Valley fold over top triangle layer and repeat Steps 4–6 on the other side.

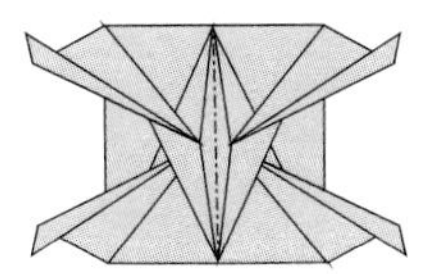

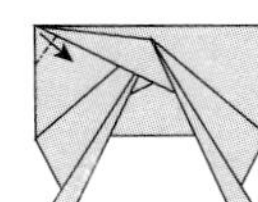

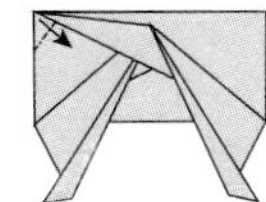

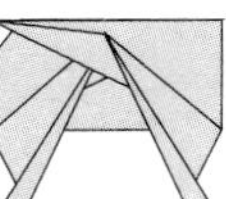

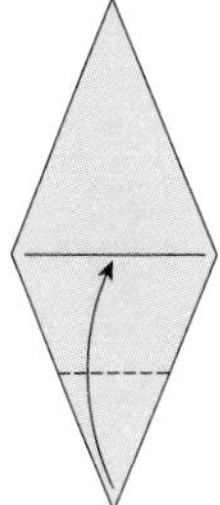

8. Mountain fold entire body and rotate model 90°.

9. Inside reverse fold to round the rump.

10. Completed zebra body.

11. Make the head: Using the smaller paper and starting with the fish base back side up, valley fold bottom point to the center crease.

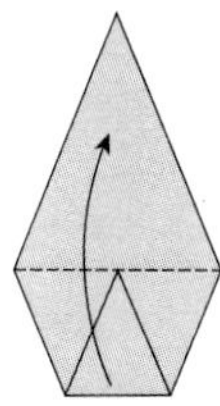

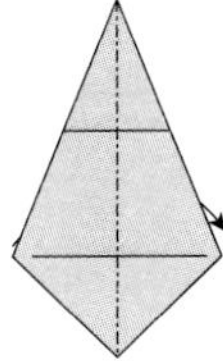

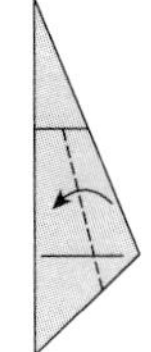

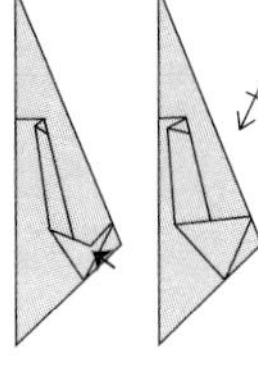

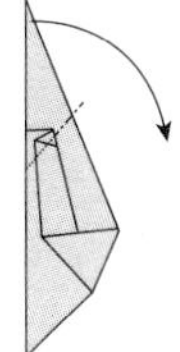

12. Valley fold bottom up along center crease.

13. Mountain fold entire model.

14. Open up top layer. Squash fold base into a triangle. Repeat squash fold on the other side.

15. Inside reverse fold inner layer of head.

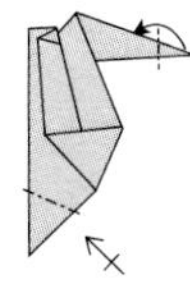

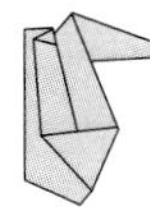

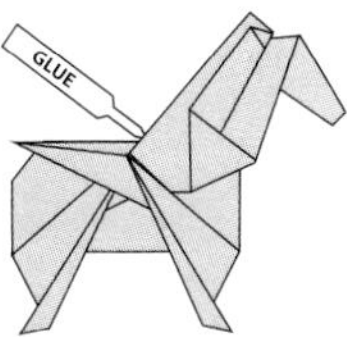

16. Inside reverse fold tip of nose. Tuck bottom of neck inside on both sides.

17. Completed head.

18. Open up head layers and place them outside the body. Tuck loose ends of the head piece into the pockets formed by the legs. Glue head to body.

TROPICAL FISH

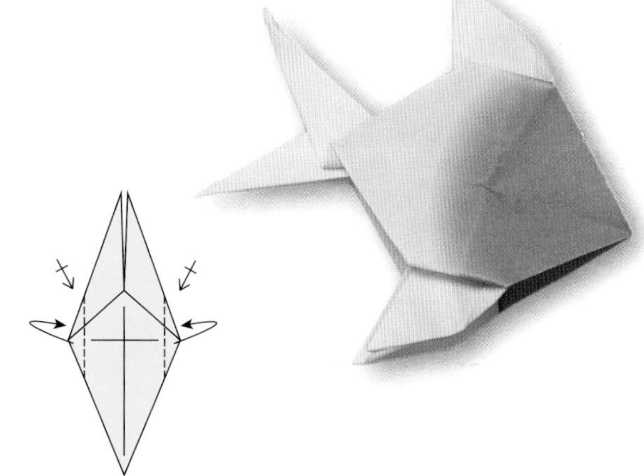

What to Use

- **6x6-inch paper =** 3-inch fish
- **3x3-inch paper =** 1½-inch fish
- **Base required:** fish (see page 14)
- **Paper required:** one sheet

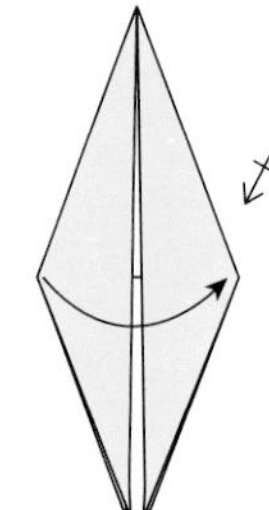

1. Starting with a bird base, valley fold over the top layer. Repeat on the other side.

2. Valley fold edges inside. Repeat on the other side.

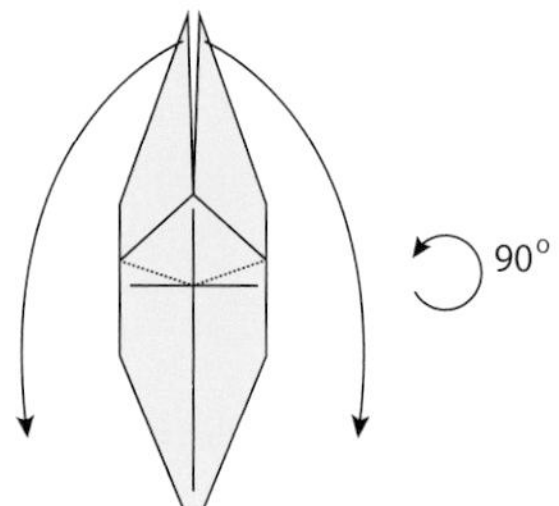

3. Inside reverse fold as far back as the paper will let you go. You want the fins to begin where the parallel edges start. Rotate the model 90°.

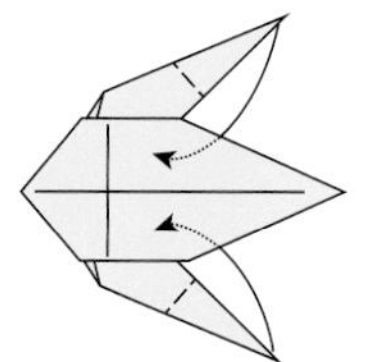

4. Outside reverse fold the fin inside to the indicated area.

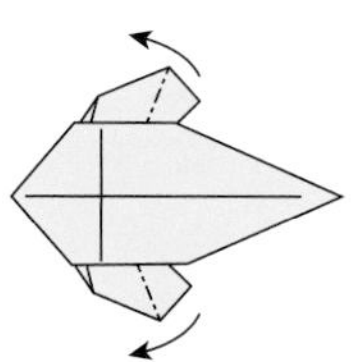

5. Inside reverse fold along the edge you just created.

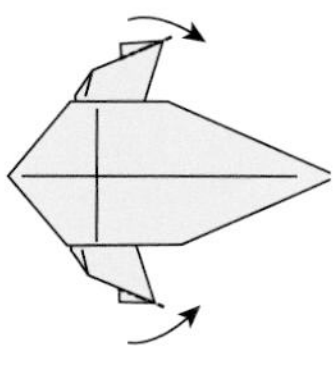

6. Inside reverse fold the fin tips.

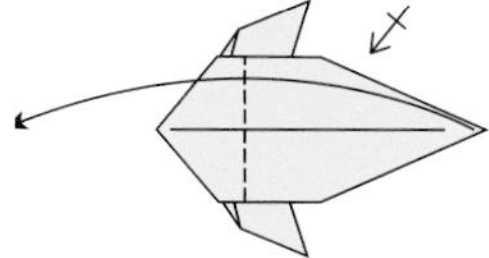

7. Valley fold tail fin along the vertical crease as shown. Repeat on other side.

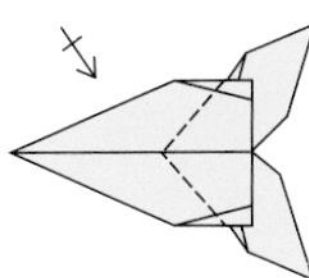

8. Valley fold top layer along the edge of the fish's face. Repeat on other side.

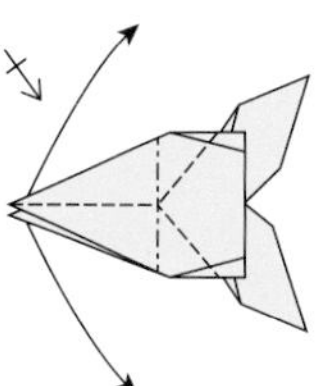

9. With the valley fold created in Step 8, rabbit ear the tail fin. Make the upper tail fin go in the opposite direction of the lower tail fin.

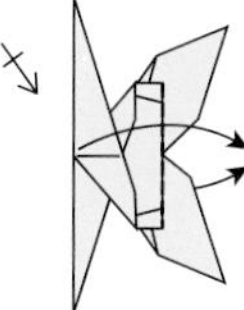

10. Fold the back half of the body to its original position.

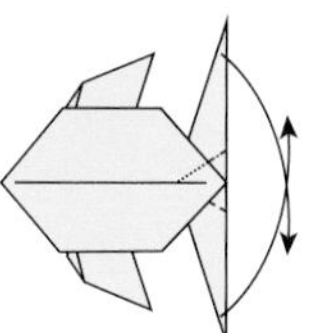

11. Mountain fold the upper tail fin and valley fold the lower tail fin.

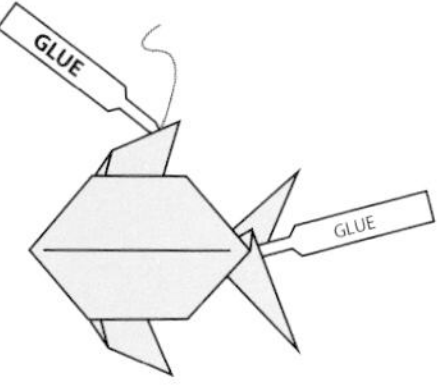

12. Glue the tail fins together, and glue the two points of the top fin together.

SEAHORSE

What to Use

- **6x6-inch paper =** 4½-inch seahorse
- **3x3-inch paper =** 2-inch seahorse
- **Base required:** fish (see page 14)
- **Paper required:** one sheet

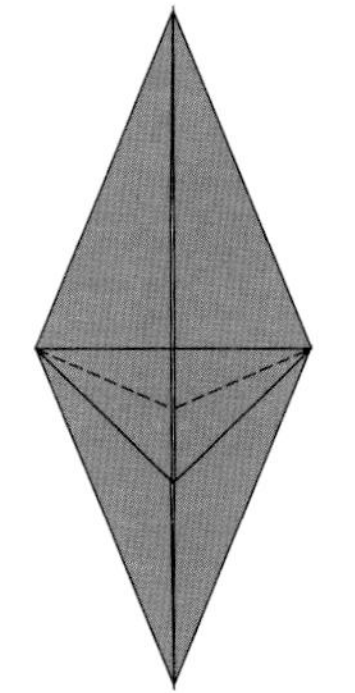

1. Starting with a fish base, valley fold to meet the horizontal center crease.

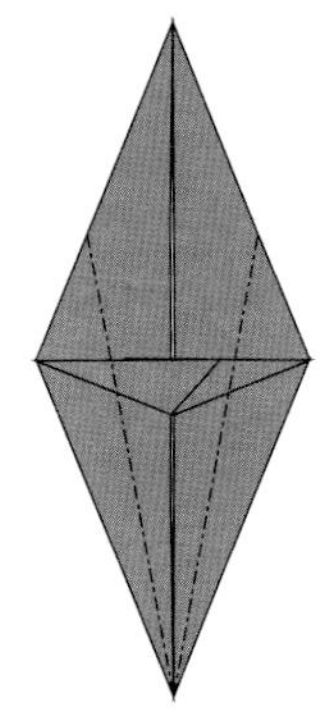

2. Mountain fold to narrow the tail.

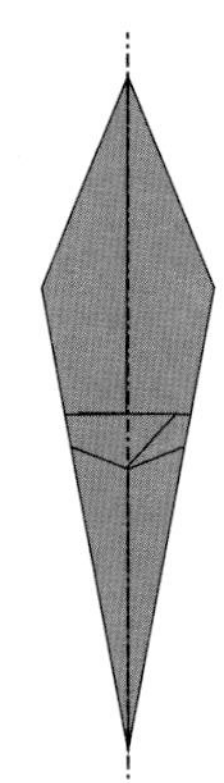

3. Mountain fold entire model along center crease.

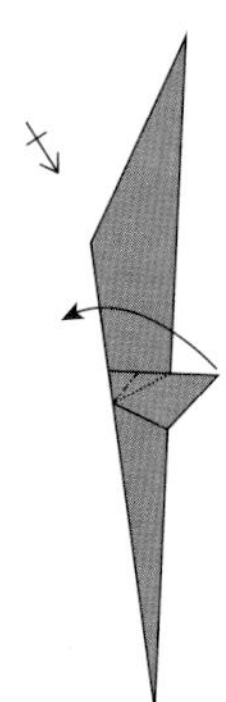

4. Pull tip of fin over to the left, creating the two creases seen here (the fin sort of falls into place). Repeat behind.

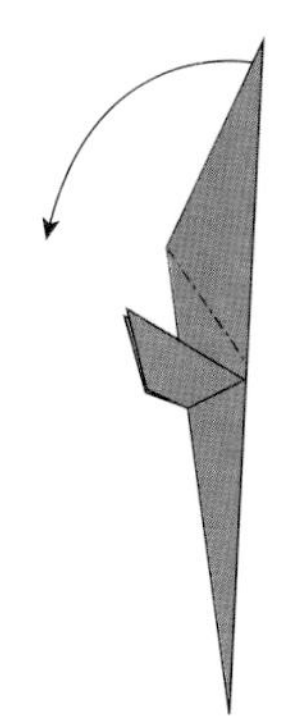

5. Inside reverse fold.

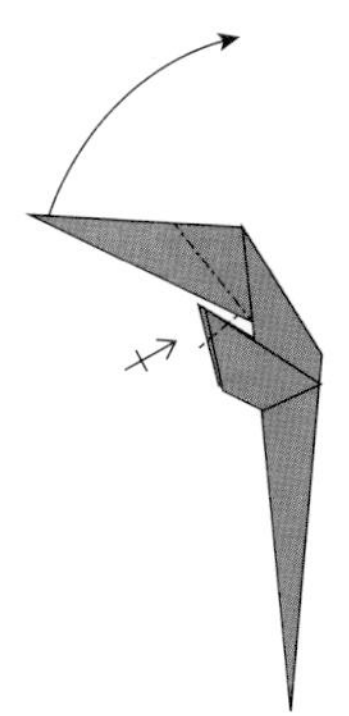

6. Inside reverse fold the head and both fin tips.

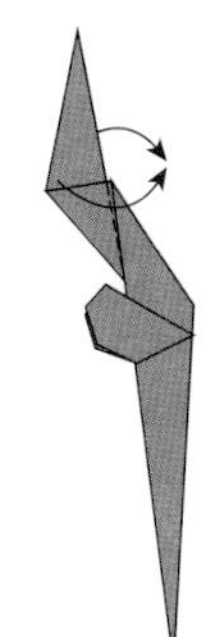

7. Outside reverse fold the head.

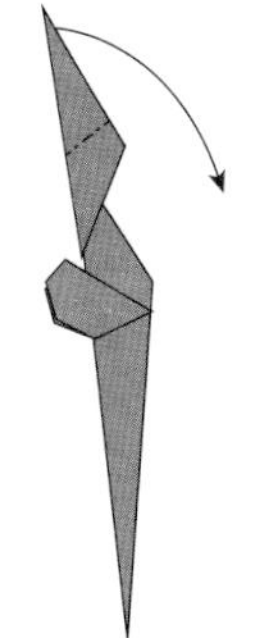

8. Inside reverse fold the head.

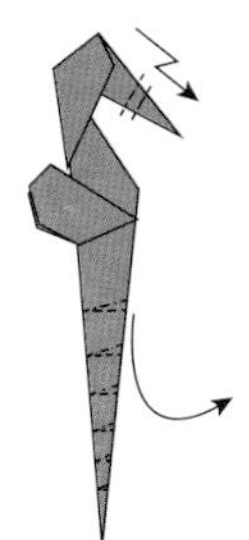

9. Pleat fold the face, and crimp fold the tail into segments. Each segment tucks into the previous segment.

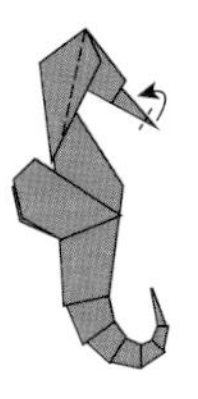

10. Inside reverse fold tip of the snout, and valley fold the earflaps.

LOBSTER

What to Use

- **6x6-inch paper =** 4-inch lobster
- **3x3-inch paper =** 4-inch lobster
- **Base required:** waterbomb (see page 13)
- **Paper required:** one sheet

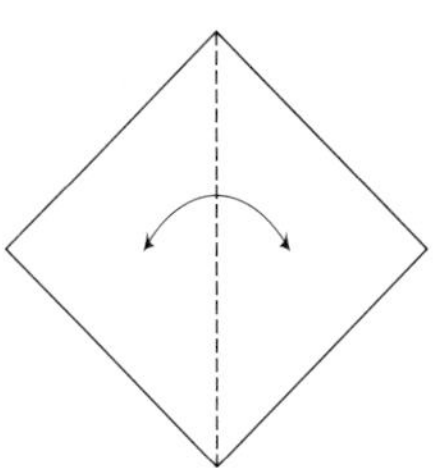

1. Starting with a flat piece of paper, valley fold and unfold to form a crease.

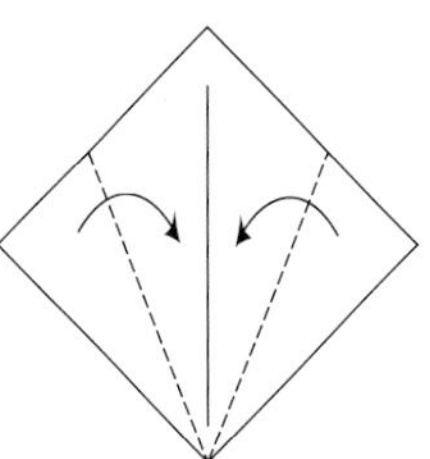

2. Valley fold sides in toward center crease.

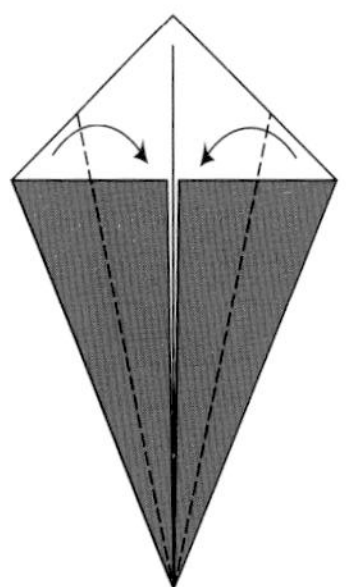

3. Valley fold sides in toward center.

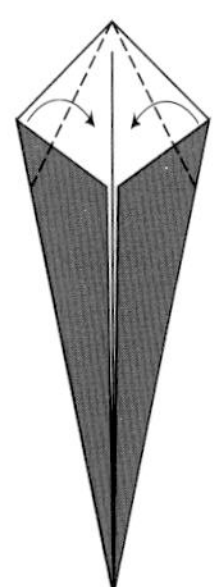

4. Valley fold upper corners as shown.

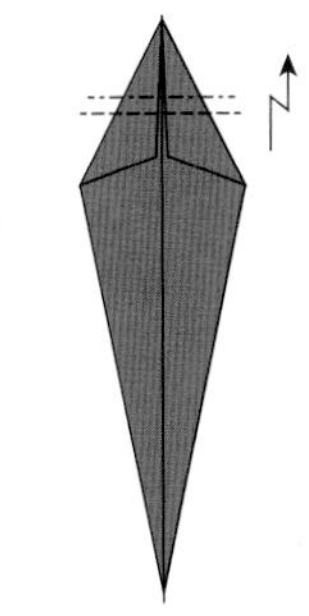

5. Pleat fold.

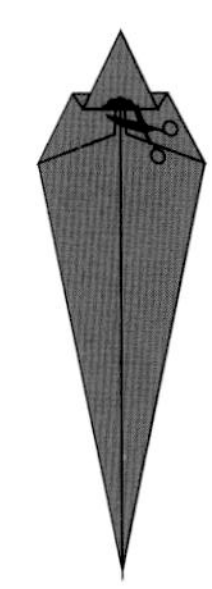

6. Use scissors to cut a hole through the top layer for the feelers. Unfold model to Step 3.

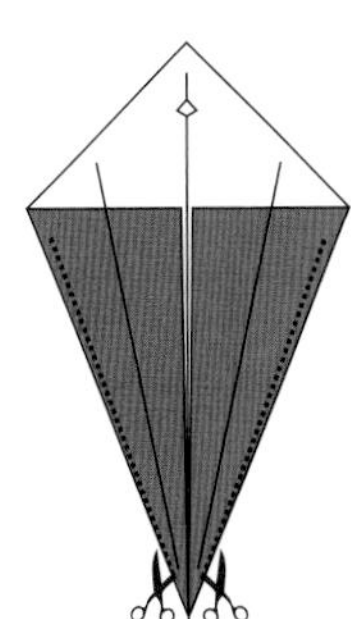

7. Trim along the dotted lines as shown to cut feelers from the body of the lobster. (Do not cut all the way through—the feelers should be attached to the body at the top end.)

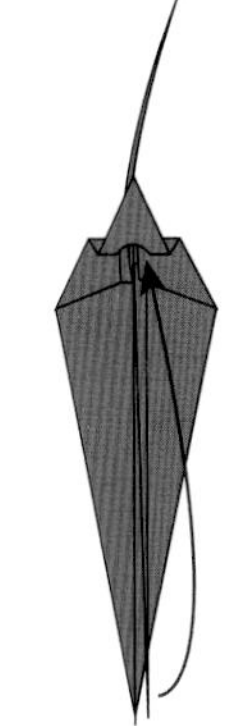

8. Fold the model back to Step 6, and then tuck feelers into the hole.

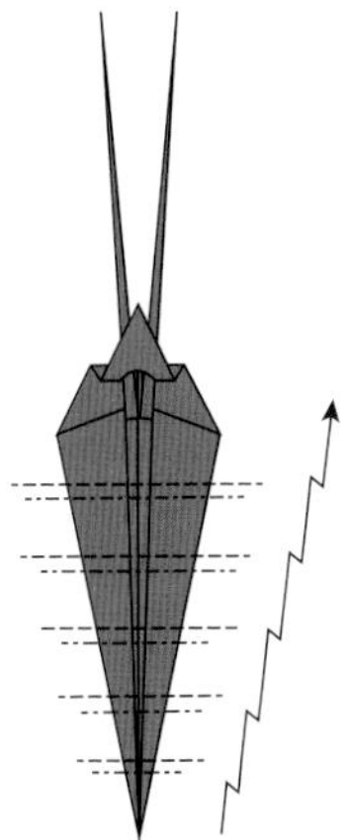

9. Pleat fold the entire body to create body segments.

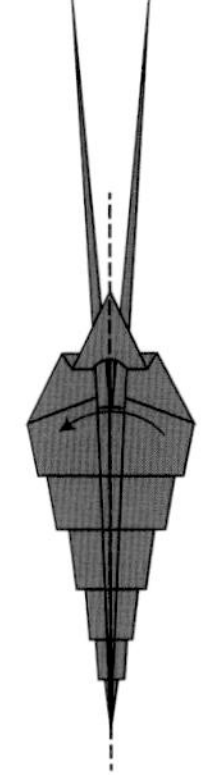

10. Valley fold model along center crease.

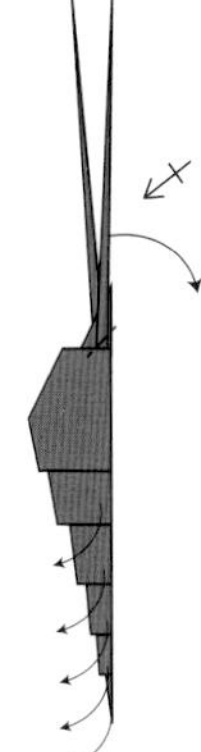

11. Valley fold feelers back and pull each pleated segment out slightly to curve the body.

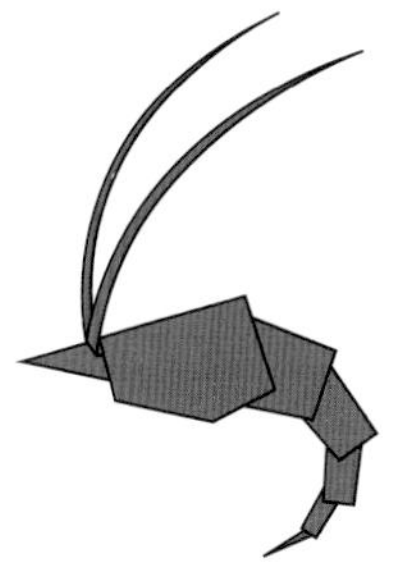

12. Completed lobster.

DRAGONFLY

What to Use

- **6x6-inch paper =** 4-inch dragonfly
- **3x3-inch paper =** 2 1/2-inch dragonfly
- **Base required:** bird (see page 12)
- **Paper required:** one sheet

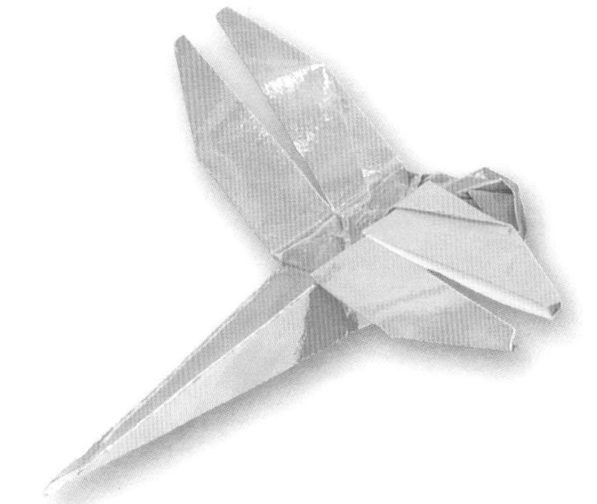

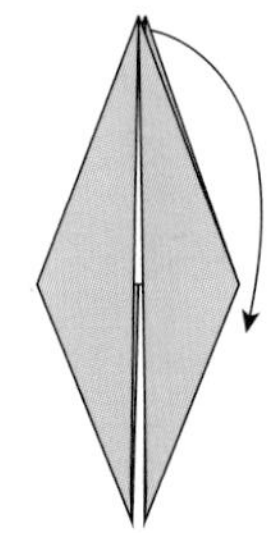

1. Starting with a bird base, mountain fold back flap down.

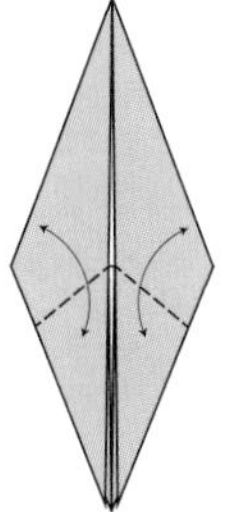

2. Valley fold and unfold to form creases.

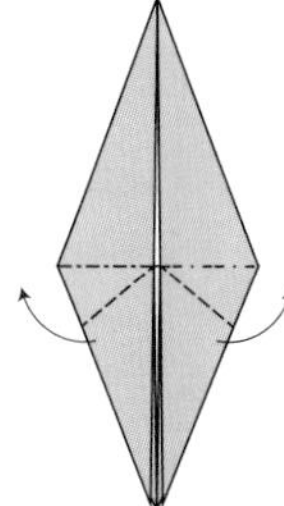

3. Using the creases you made, valley fold the two bottom flaps out and up.

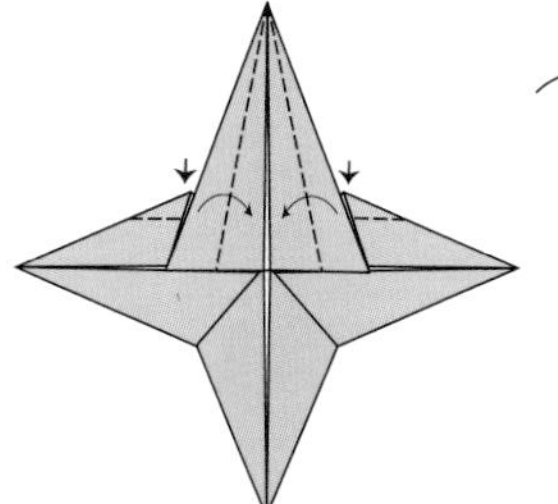

4. Valley fold to make the tail thinner. Squash fold the edges where indicated by the arrows to form the wings.

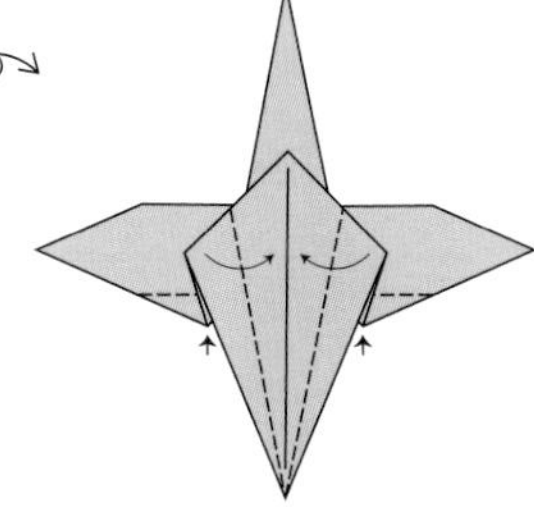

5. Turn the model over and repeat Step 4 at the other end of the dragonfly.

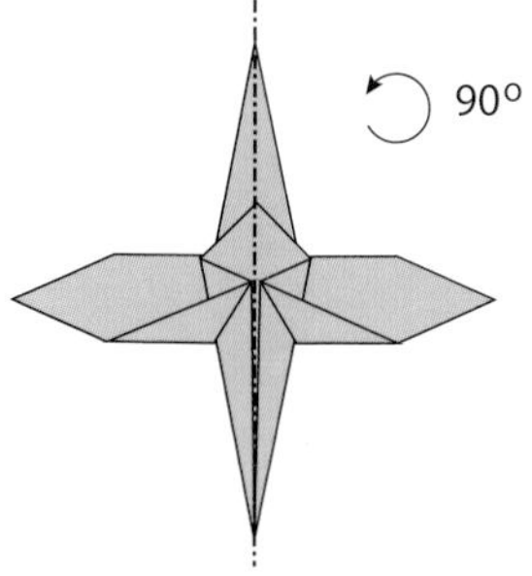

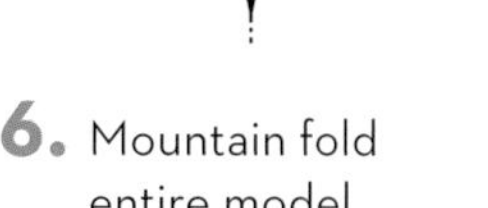

6. Mountain fold entire model. Rotate model 90°.

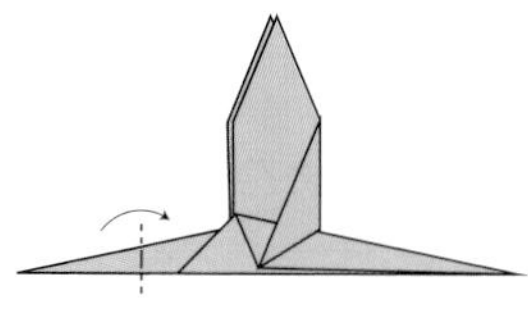

7. Inside reverse fold to begin forming the head.

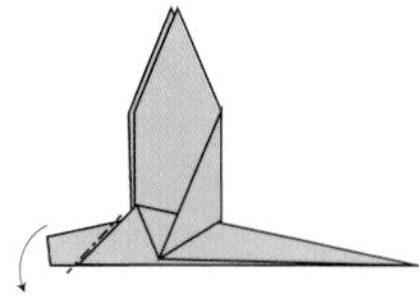

8. Outside reverse fold to finish forming the head.

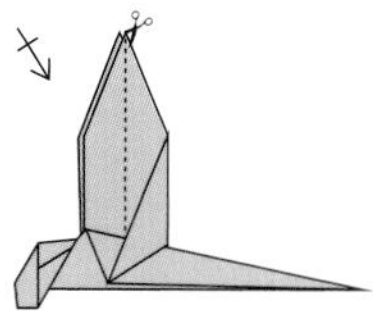

9. Cut each wing into two halves.

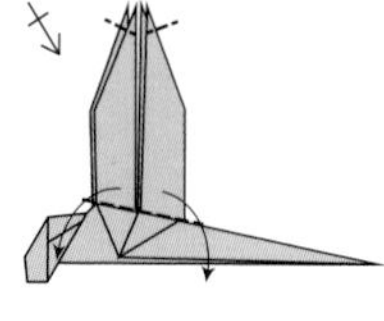

10. Mountain fold the wings down. Inside reverse fold the wing tips.

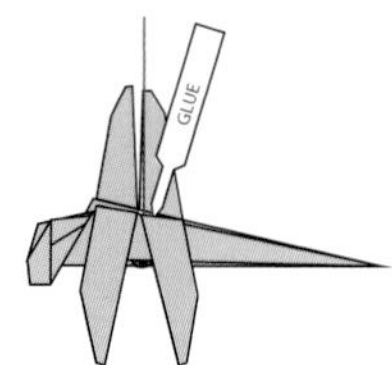

11. Apply glue to the center of the dragonfly to keep the body together and to assist with proper balance.

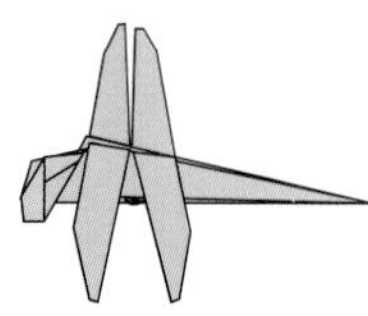

12. Completed dragonfly

FROG

What to Use

- **6x6-inch paper =** $2\,^3/_4$-inch frog
- **Base required:** frog (see page 15)
- **Paper required:** one sheet

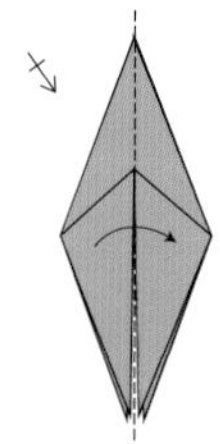

1. Starting with a frog base, valley fold the top layer over. Repeat on other side.

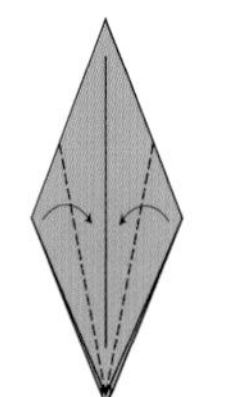

2. Valley fold sides in toward center. Repeat on all faces of the model.

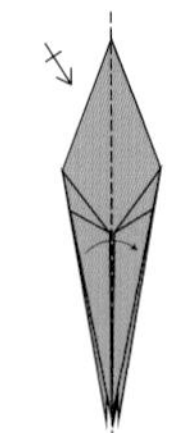

3. Valley fold top layer. Repeat on other side so you can see the split between the legs.

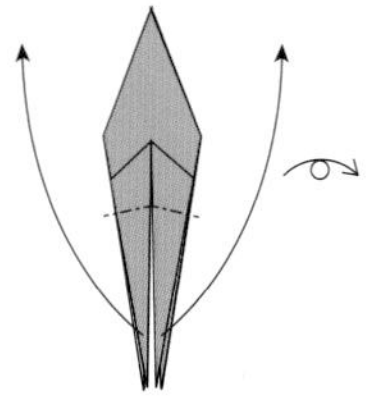

4. Inside reverse fold top layer to form forelegs. Flip model over.

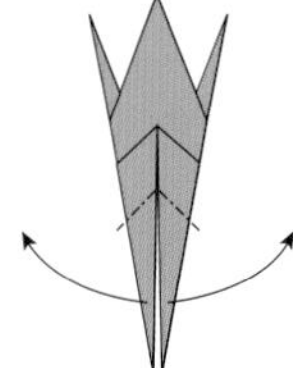

5. Inside reverse fold top layer to form back legs.

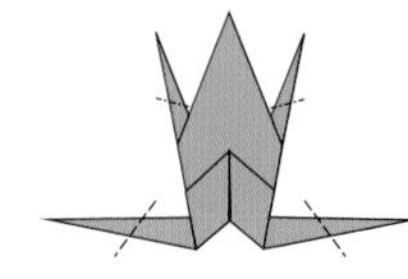

6. Inside reverse fold all limbs to create joints.

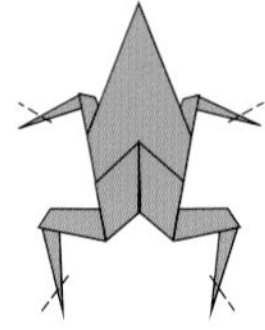

7. Inside reverse fold to create feet.

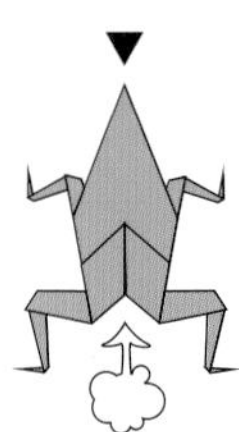

8. While pressing down on its nose, inflate the frog by carefully blowing air into the hole at the rear.

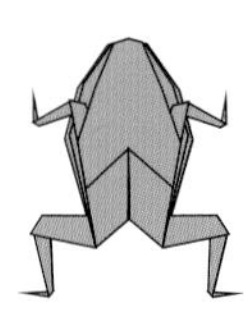

9. Completed frog.

DUCK

What to Use

- **6x6-inch paper =** 3½-inch duck
- **3x3-inch paper =** 1¾-inch duck
- **Paper required:** one sheet

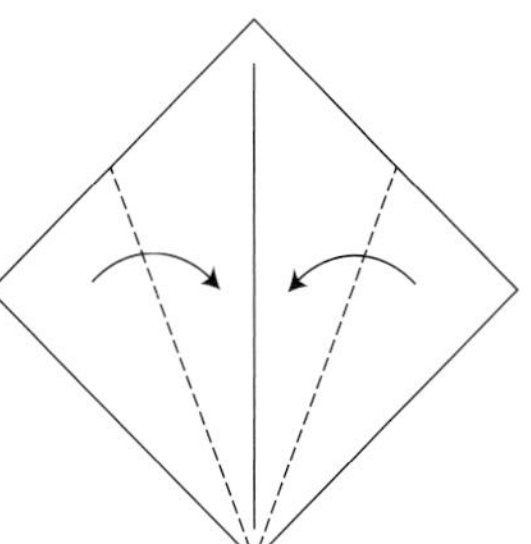

1. Crease center and then valley fold sides.

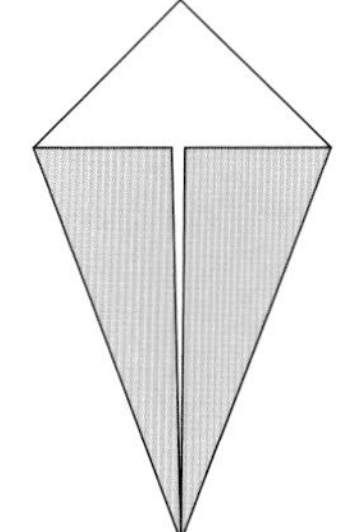

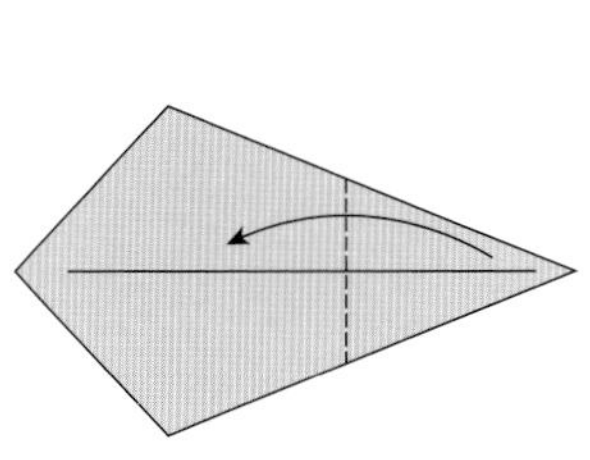

2. Rotate model 90° and flip it over.

3. Valley fold to form the duck's neck.

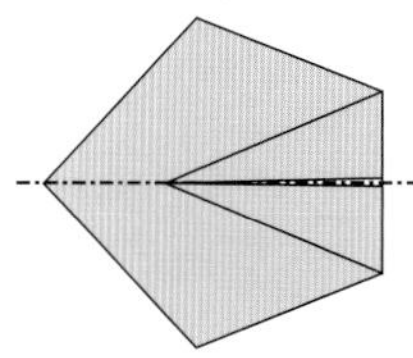

4. Mountain fold entire model.

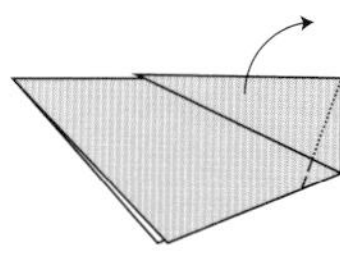

5. Pull the neck up slightly.

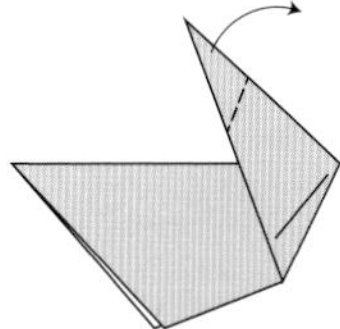

6. Outside reverse fold to form head.

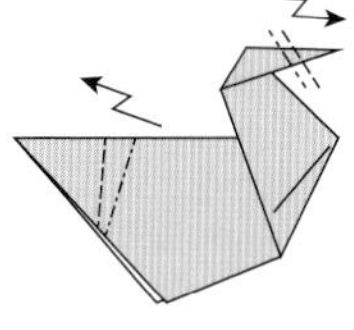

7. Pleat fold beak and tail.

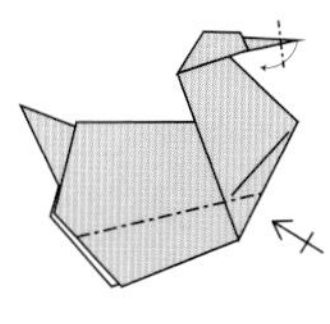

8. Inside reverse fold beak. Mountain fold bottom of duck using previous neck crease as a guide. Repeat on other side.

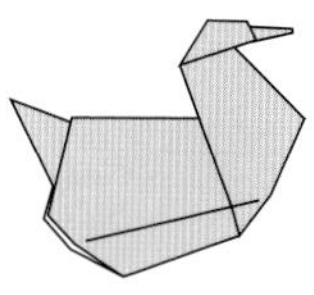

9. Completed duck.

PENGUIN

What to Use

- **6x6-inch paper =** 4½-inch penguin
- **3x3-inch paper =** 2¼-inch penguin
- **Base required:** fish (see page 14)
- **Paper required:** one sheet

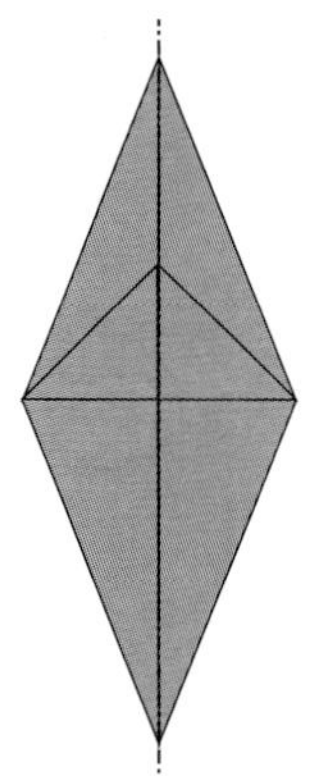

1. Starting with a fish base, mountain fold the entire model along the vertical crease.

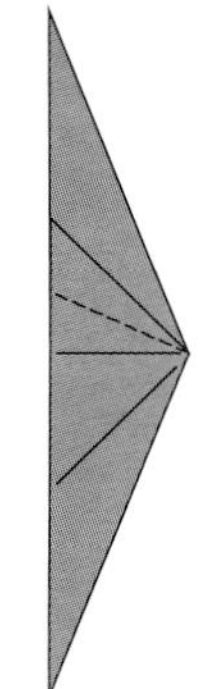

2. Valley fold flap down so it meets the horizontal crease.

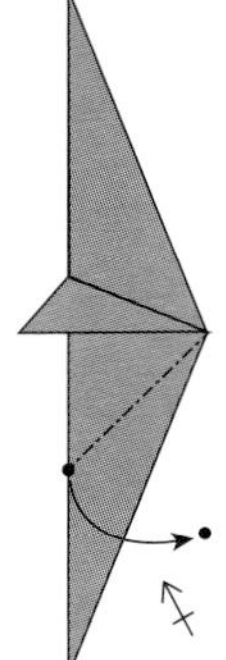

3. Using the dots on the diagram as a guide, mountain fold and pull top layer out so that mountain fold meets the dot. The flipper will follow as you pull the paper down. Repeat on the other side.

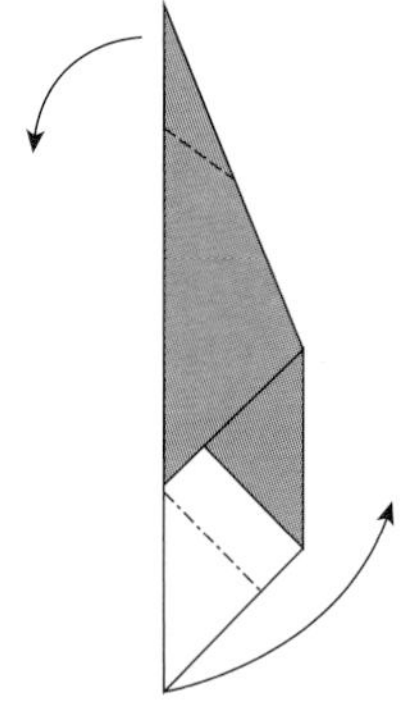

4. Outside reverse fold head. Inside reverse fold tail.

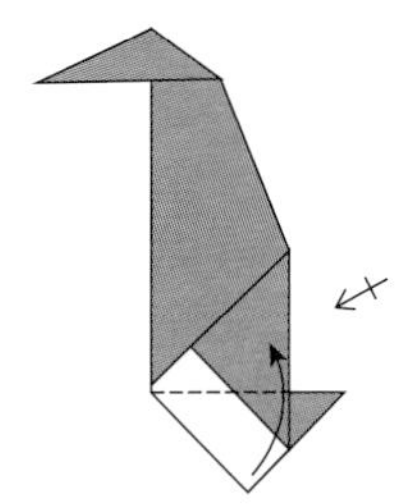

5. Valley fold the feet up on both sides.

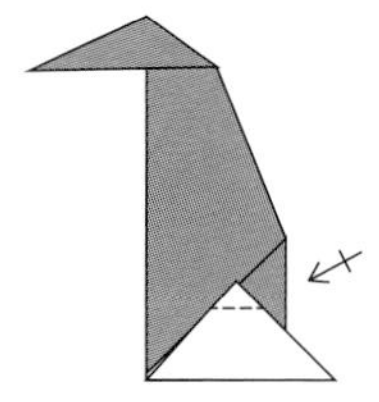

6. Valley fold the tip of the foot down. Repeat on the other side.

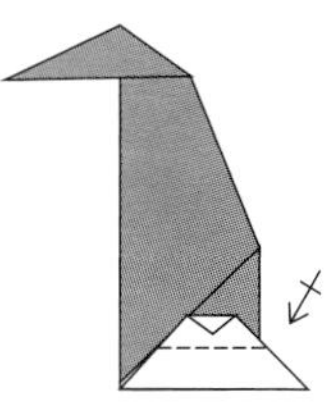

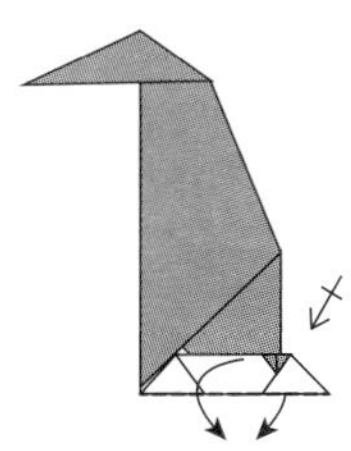

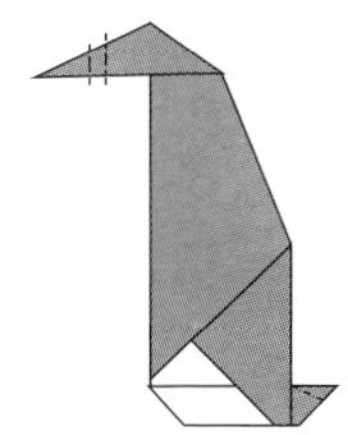

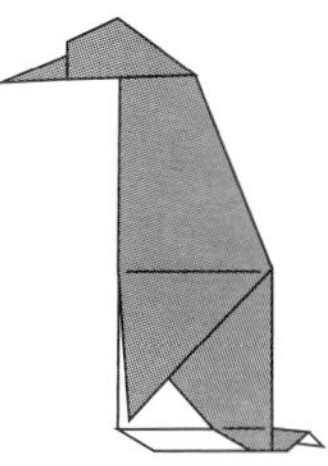

7. Valley fold the foot down so it meets the bottom edge of the penguin. Repeat on the other side.

8. Fold the finished foot down. Repeat on the other side. The penguin should be able to stand on its own feet once the model is completed.

9. Pleat fold the head to form the beak. Inside reverse fold the tip of the tail.

10. Completed penguin.

6-POINT STAR

What to Use

- **6x6-inch paper =** 3-inch star
- **3x3-inch paper =** $1\frac{1}{2}$-inch star
- **Paper required:** one sheet

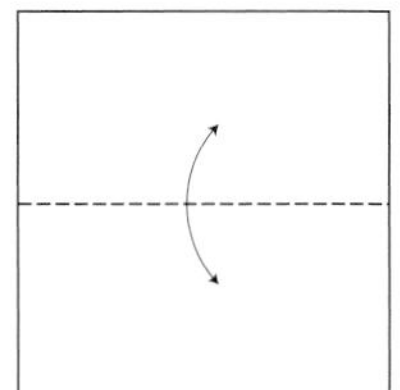

1. Make an equilateral triangle: Valley fold paper square in half. Crease and open up.

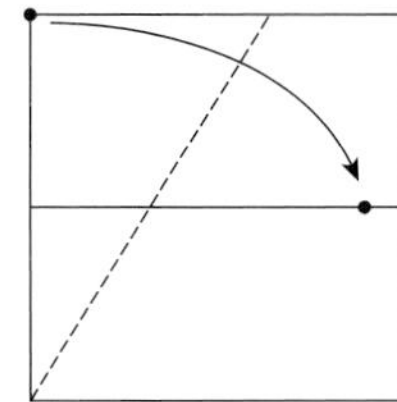

2. Valley fold so that the top left corner meets the center fold and the bottom left corner remains sharp. Use the dots in the diagram as a guide.

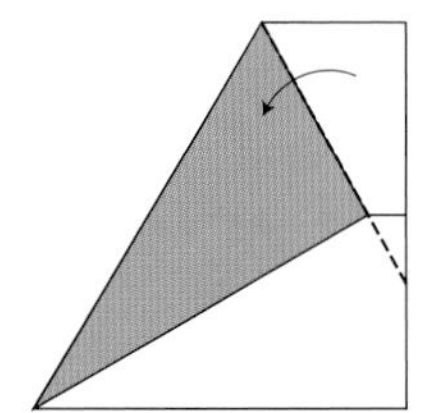

3. Valley fold down along edge of fold made in Step 2.

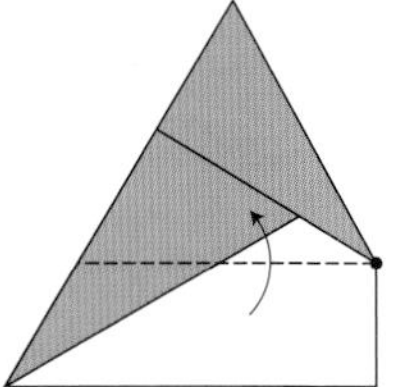

4. Valley fold up, beginning where the right triangle meets the edge, as indicated by the dot in the diagram.

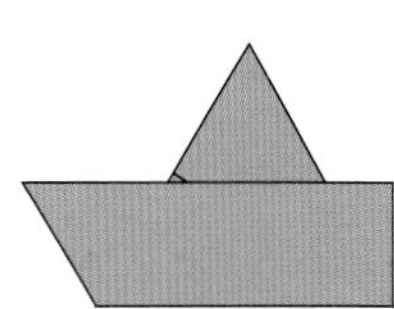

5. Crease well, then open up all your folds.

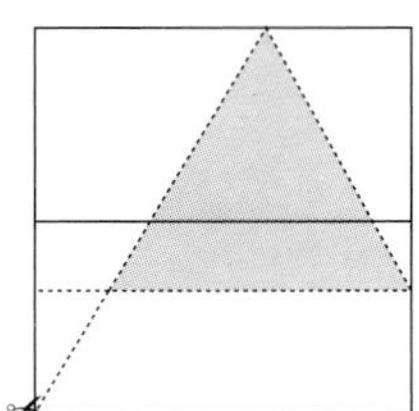

6. Cut along the creases that form your equilateral triangle.

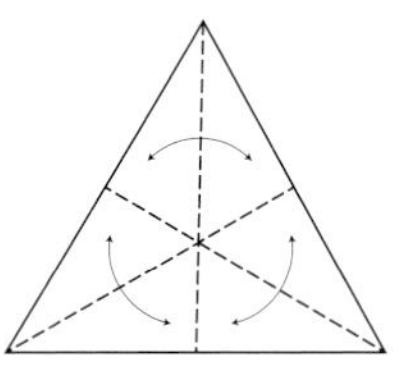

7. Valley fold, crease, and unfold.

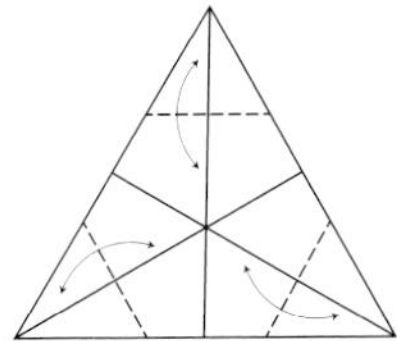

8. Valley fold all corners to the center point, crease, and unfold.

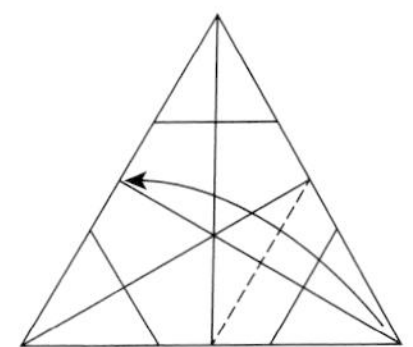

9. Valley fold one corner to center of far side.

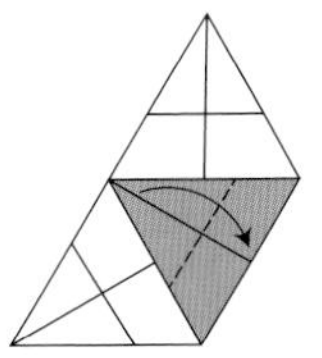

10. Valley fold the point of that corner back along existing crease.

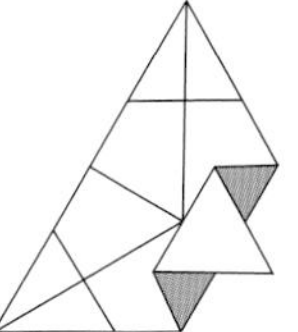

11. Repeat Steps 9 and 10 on remaining corners.

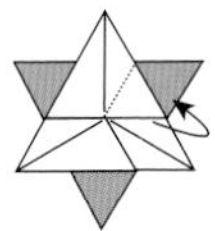

12. Pull corner of flap from behind.

13. Your star should look like this from above... and like this from below.

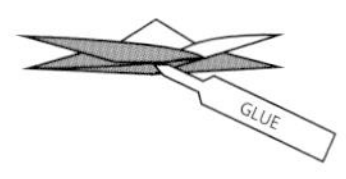

14. Apply glue between layers so star stays flat.

POP-UP STAR

WHAT TO USE

- **6x6-inch paper =** 5-inch star
- **3x3-inch paper =** 2½-inch star
- **Base required:** blintz (see page 14)
- **Paper required:** one sheet

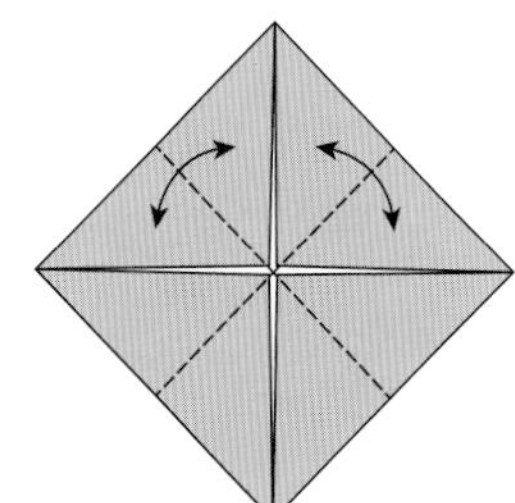

1. By beginning with a bintz base, you create an additional layer of paper required for the three dimensionality of this star. Valley fold and unfold to crease.

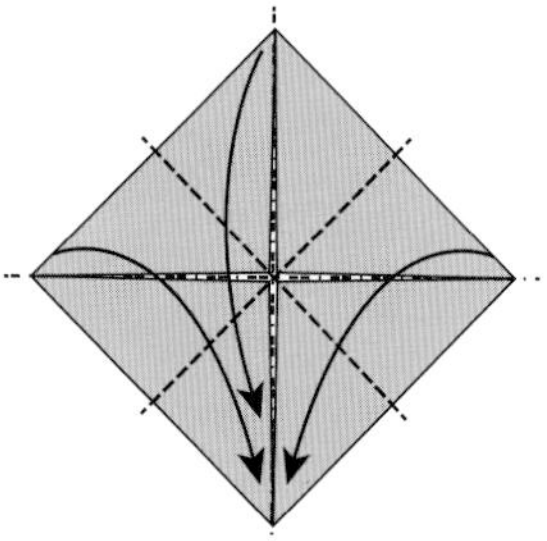

2. Using alternating mountain and valley folds along existing creases, collapse the blintz base into a square base.

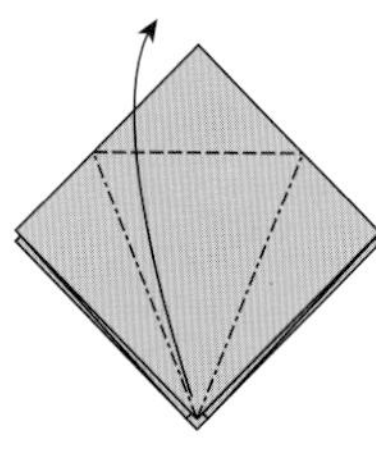

3. Petal fold front and back to form a bird base.

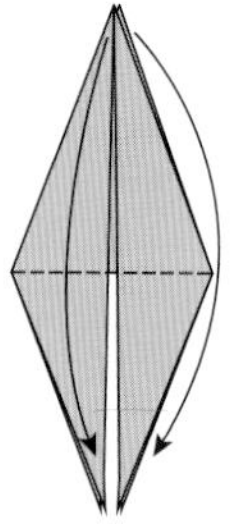

4. Valley fold front and back flaps down.

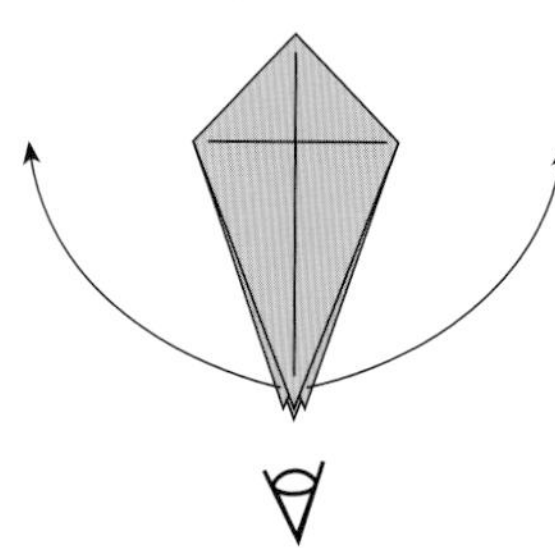

5. Pull middle points up and out creating a stretched bird base.

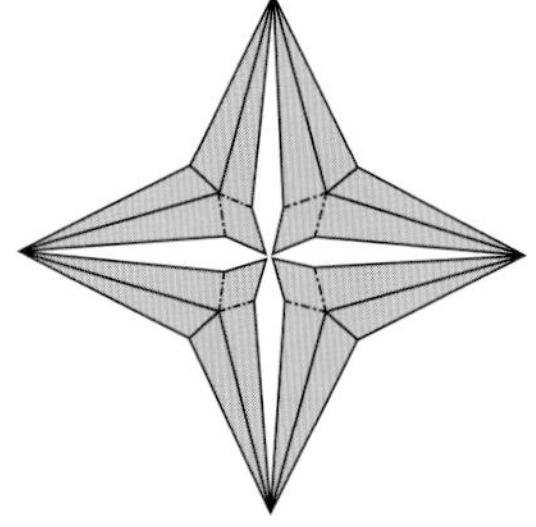

6. Make tiny mountain folds along the existing creases near the center of the star, as shown. These creases should be sharp.

WATERBOMB

WHAT TO USE

- **6x6-inch paper =** $1\frac{1}{2}$-inch waterbomb
- **3x3-inch paper =** $\frac{3}{4}$-inch waterbomb
- **Base required:** waterbomb (see page 13)
- **Paper required:** one sheet

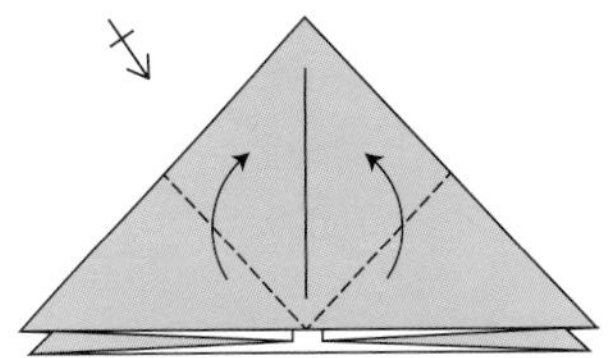

1. Starting with a waterbomb base, valley fold front flaps up to meet the top. Repeat on the other side.

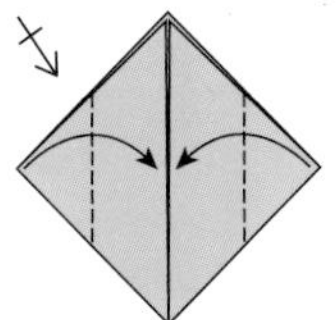

2. Valley fold front flaps to center. Repeat on the other side.

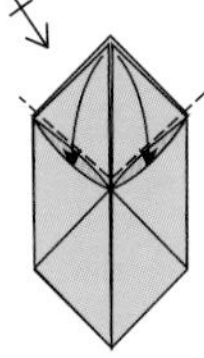

3. The flaps you just folded created pockets in which you tuck these loose ends. Repeat on the other side.

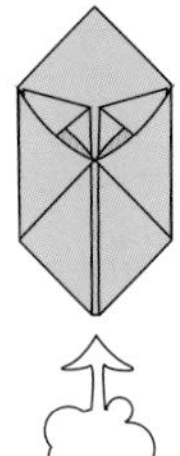

4. While supporting opposite end, inflate the model by blowing gently through the hole at the bottom. Turn model upside down.

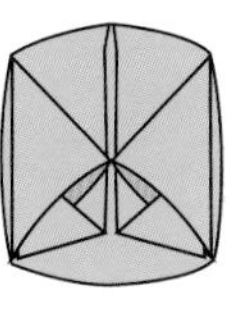

5. Completed waterbomb.

WATERBOMB BASEBALL

What to Use

- **6x6-inch paper =** 6-inch ball
- **3x3-inch paper =** 3-inch ball
- **Base required:** waterbomb (see page 13)
- **Paper required:** six sheets (for illustration purposes, this example uses three different colors)

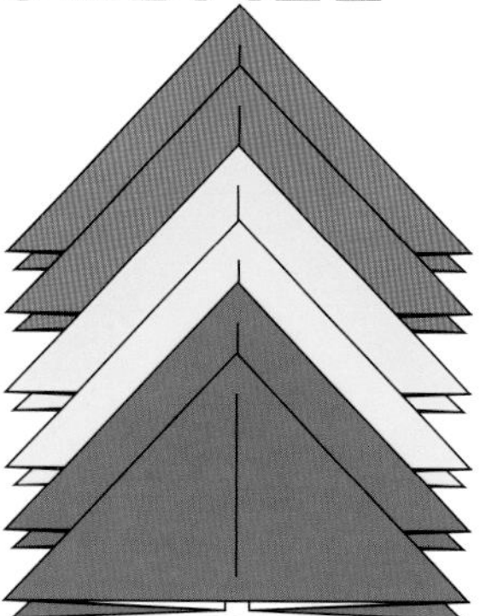

1. Start by folding six waterbomb bases.

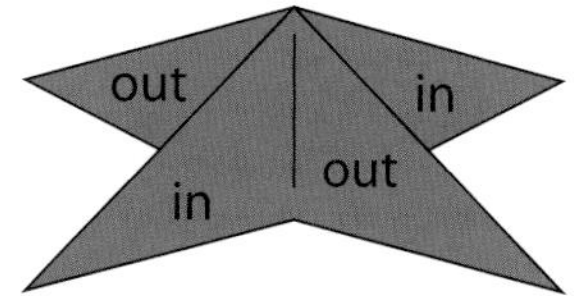

2. Crease and open up a waterbomb base as shown. Note that every base has a pair of "inside" flaps and a pair of "outside" flaps.

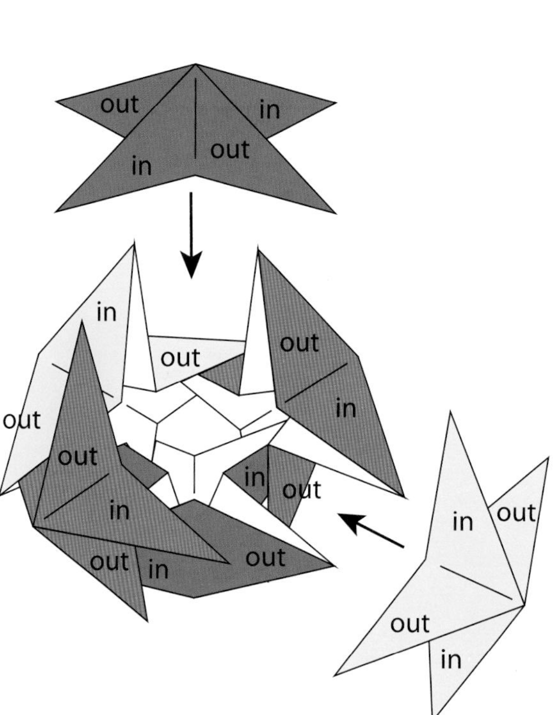

3. Assemble the ball by slipping the pieces into their corresponding locations, gently easing the "inside" flaps into the pockets of the "outside" flaps.

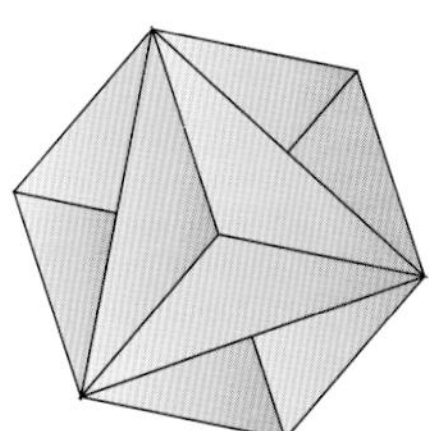
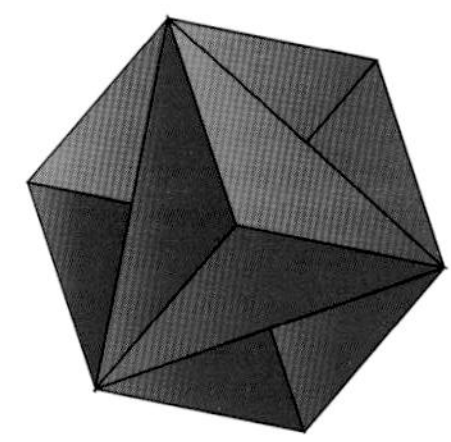
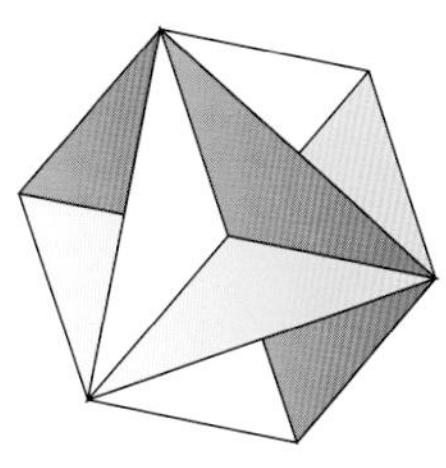
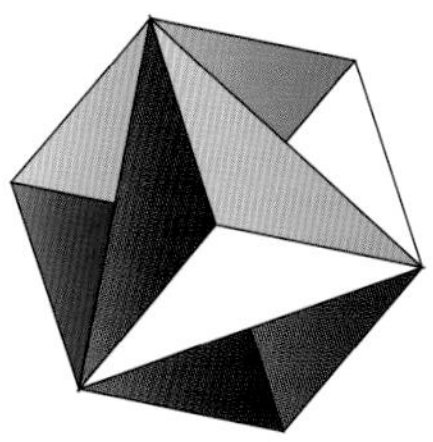

4. The design appears more complex when you experiment with color. You can use six sheets of the same color...

5. ...three sheets each of two different colors...

6. ...two sheets each of three different colors...

7. ...or six different colors, depending on the look you want.

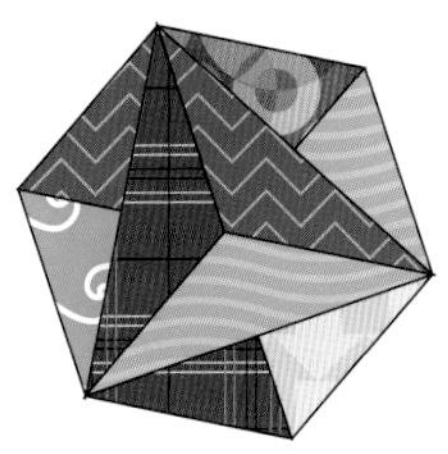

8. Using patterned paper for the waterbomb baseball can also create some interesting looks.

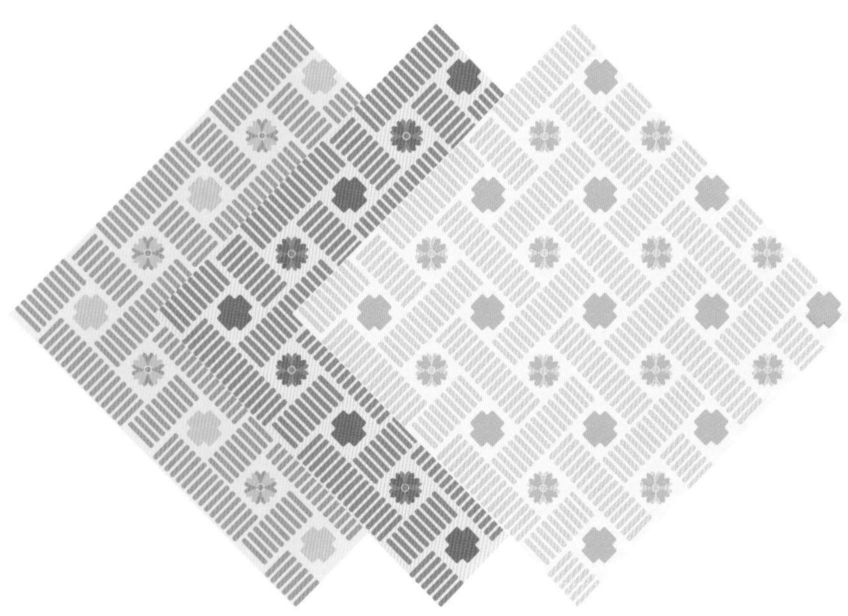

MODULAR UNIT BALL

What to Use

- **6x6-inch paper =** $2\frac{3}{4}$-inch ball
- **3x3-inch paper =** $1\frac{1}{2}$-inch ball
- **Base required:** blintz (see page 14)
- **Paper required:** six sheets of the same size paper (for illustration purposes, this example uses six different colors)

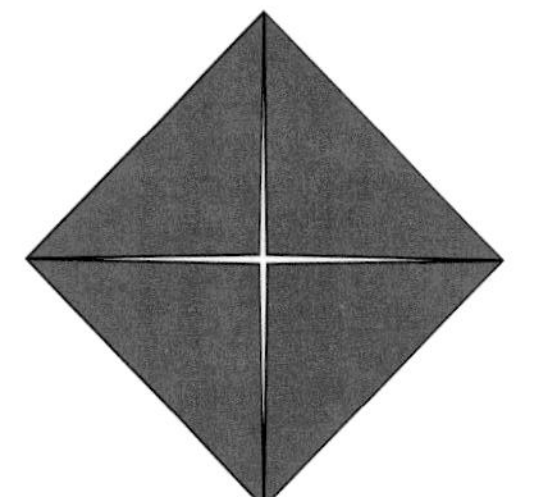

1. Starting with a blintz base, flip the model over.

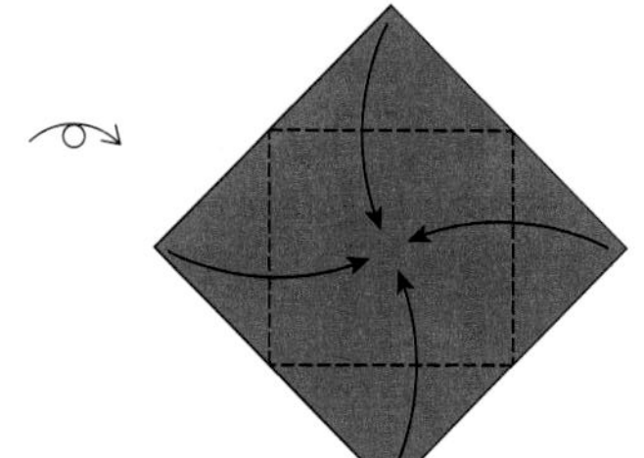

2. Valley fold points to center.

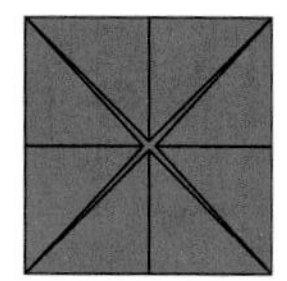

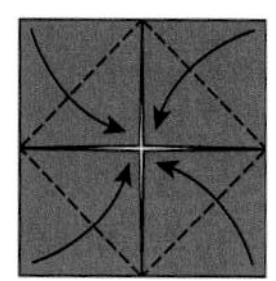

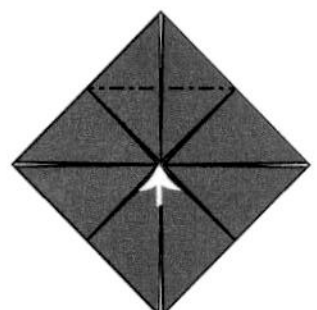

3. Flip model over.

4. Valley fold points to center again.

5. Flip model over again.

6. Slowly push the center point out and the end should squash fold into place. Repeat on three other corners.

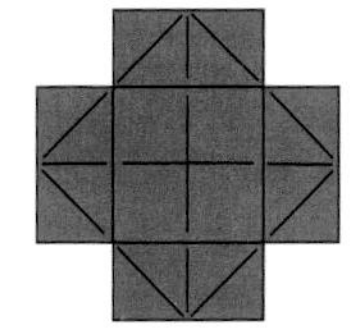

7. This is the completed unit. Make five more, following Steps 1–6 above.

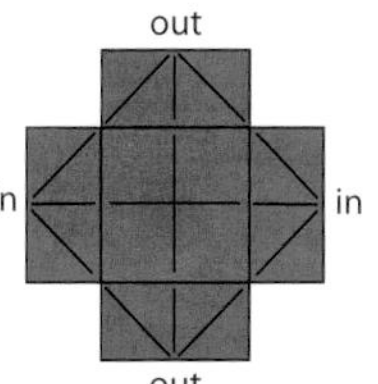

8. Note that each unit has a pair of "inside" flaps and a pair of "outside" flaps.

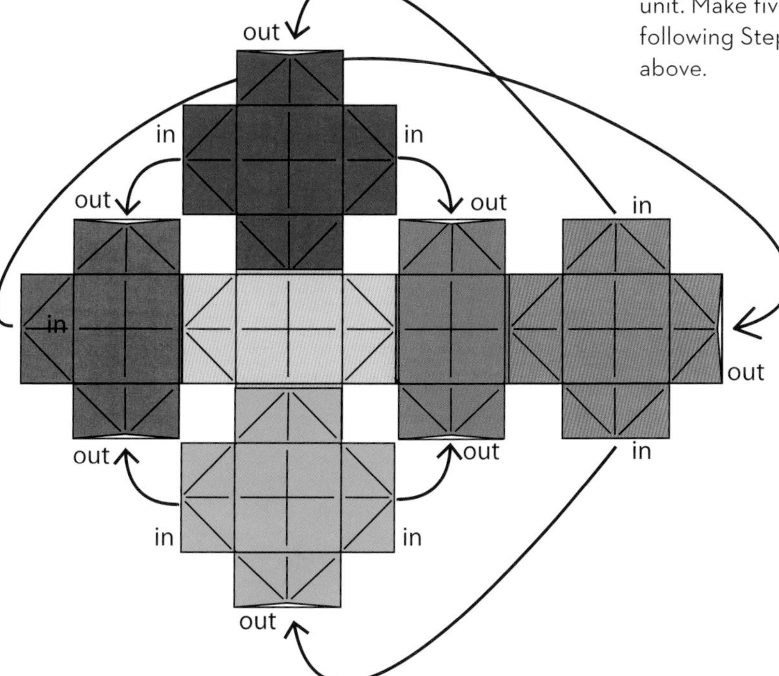

9. Assemble the model starting with the central unit (the yellow unit in the diagram). Notice that the right and left "outside" flaps of the central unit are visible and the top and bottom "inside" flaps of the central unit are now tucked into the "outside" flaps of the units above and below. Take your time with this assembly, gently easing the units into place.

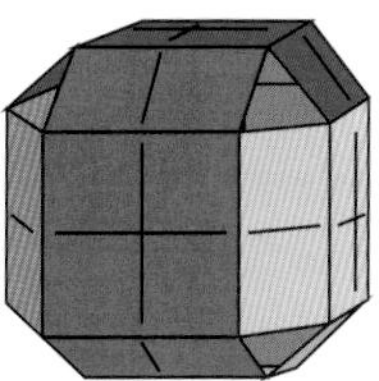

10. Completed Modular Unit Ball

HEXAHEDRON

What to Use

- **6x6-inch paper =** 3-inch hexahedron
- **3x3-inch paper =** 1½-inch hexahedron
- **Paper required:** three sheets of same size paper (for illustration purposes, the example below uses three different colors)

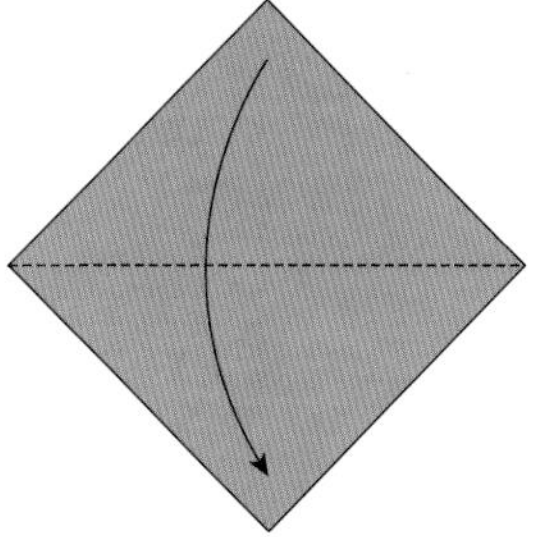

1. Valley fold one sheet of paper in half so the color you want seen stays on the outside.

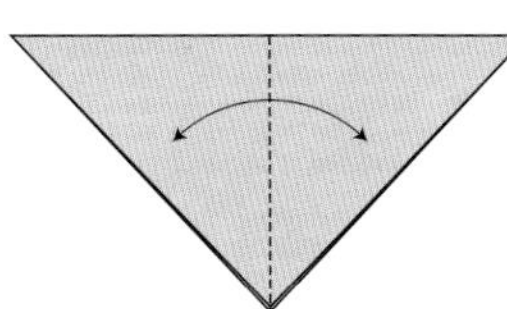

2. Valley fold and unfold to crease well.

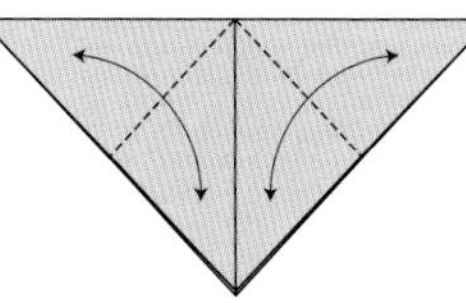

3. Valley fold and unfold to crease well.

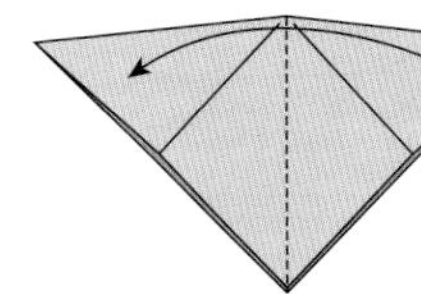

4. Valley fold in half again along the crease made in Step 2.

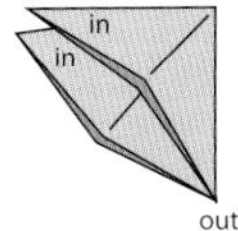

5. The completed unit. Make two more units following Steps 1–4 above. Note that each unit has two "inside" points and one "outside" point.

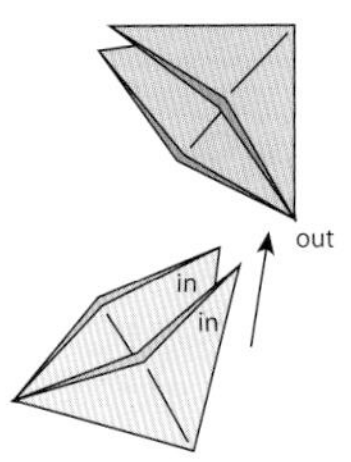

6. Begin with two units. Insert the two free "inside" points into the pockets of an opposite "outside" point.

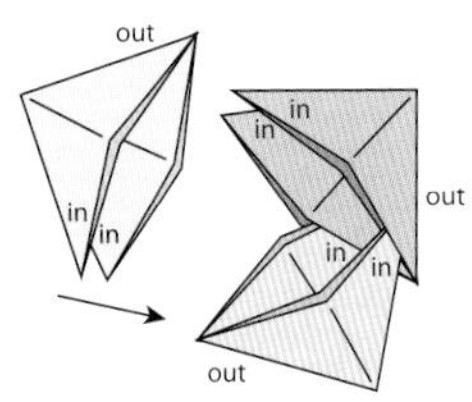

7. Add the third unit in the same way, easing the points into place.

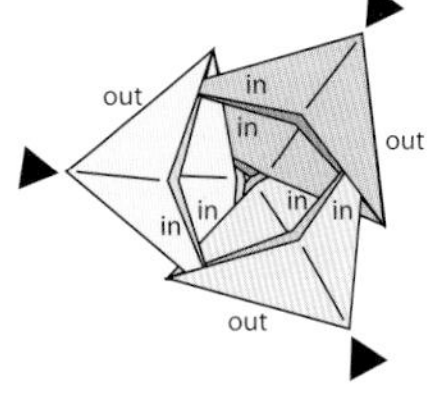

8. Gently push all three units together so they hold together firmly.

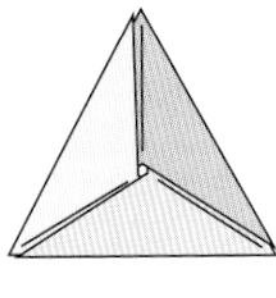

9. This is the completed model. Notice the small hole in the very center.